THE ASCENDED CHRIST

THE ASCENDED CHRIST

A STUDY IN
THE EARLIEST CHRISTIAN TEACHING

BY

HENRY BARCLAY SWETE, D.D.

EMERITUS PROFESSOR OF DIVINITY IN THE UNIVERSITY OF CAMBRIDGE
HON. CANON OF ELY; HON. CHAPLAIN TO THE KING

πορεύομαι ἑτοιμάσαι τόπον ὑμῖν

WIPF & STOCK · Eugene, Oregon

Wipf and Stock Publishers
199 W 8th Ave, Suite 3
Eugene, OR 97401

The Ascended Christ
A Study in the Earliest Christian Teaching
By Swete, Henry Barclay
ISBN 13: 978-1-55635-748-0
ISBN 10: 1-55635-748-6
Publication date 12/3/2007
Previously published by Macmillan and Co., 1922

TO THE MEMORY OF
C. A. S. S. AND A. R. S.

ΜΕΓΑ ἐστὶν τὸ τῆς εὐσεβείας μυστήριον, ὃς
    ἐφανερώθη ἐν σαρκί,
    ἐδικαιώθη ἐν πνεύματι,
        ὤφθη ἀγγέλοις·
    ἐκηρύχθη ἐν ἔθνεσιν,
    ἐπιστεύθη ἐν κόσμῳ,
        ἀνελήμφθη ἐν δόξῃ.

FOREWORD

THIS little book has been written as a sequel to *Appearances of our Lord after the Passion*. Like its predecessor, it has grown out of a course of lectures given to candidates for Holy Orders. My hope is that in its present form it may be of some service to the younger clergy, and also to the increasing class of Church workers among the laity. The subject is one which, I am persuaded, ought to be kept prominently before the minds of those who take part in Christian work of any kind, and indeed of all whose ambition it is to live their lives in Christ.

The Resurrection of our Lord would have been an event of comparatively small significance from the standpoint of the religious life, if it had been no more than a return to life on earth for a shorter or a longer space of time. Its supreme importance lies in this, that it was the first stage of His withdrawal into the spiritual order, and His preparation for it. From the moment that He rose He could say, *I ascend*; the upward journey had begun.

Easter is preliminary to Ascension-tide, and Ascension-tide opens before our faith the full glory of the life of Christ with God. With that life in heaven the life of the Church on earth is inseparably bound up. I shall be thankful if these pages are permitted to set forward in any measure the revival of the great Ascension festival in parishes where the Church bell is silent or awakens a feeble response on the day when our Lord entered into His glory.

CAMBRIDGE,
Advent, 1910.

CONTENTS

		PAGE
INTRODUCTION		xi

CHAPTER		
I.	THE ASCENSION AND THE SESSION	1
II.	THE KING	16
III.	THE PRIEST	34
IV.	THE PROPHET	52
V.	THE HEAD	68
VI.	THE MEDIATOR, INTERCESSOR, AND ADVOCATE	87
VII.	THE FORERUNNER	101
VIII.	THE PRESENCE IN THE MIDST	116
IX.	THE COMING ONE	128
X.	THE JUDGE	140
POSTSCRIPT		154
INDEX		167

INTRODUCTION

1. The human life of the Incarnate Son, between the Nativity and the Return, divides itself into two unequal and dissimilar parts. The first is the short period during which the Lord lived on earth in the flesh; the second, the heavenly life, which according to our measure of time already approaches nineteen centuries. In the first He is the Christ of human history; in the second, the Christ of spiritual experience. The dividing line is the Ascension. At the moment when the Lord ascended, there lay behind Him His completed earthly life—the Infancy and the Childhood, the Manhood and the Ministry, the Crucifixion and the Resurrection; while before Him there opened the whole length of the life in heaven, which to His humanity was a new experience, bringing new fields of thought and work and an outlook on the still more splendid future reserved for Him in the ages to come.

2. Of this greater and higher life of our Lord the many 'Lives of Jesus' which are current do not treat; they stop short either at the Ascension, or before it—at the Death of the Cross. No blame can attach to their writers for limiting themselves to the earthly life, unless they assume that materials do not exist for a study of the life beyond. The Gospels draw the same limit, not assuredly from an agnostic reserve, but because for obvious reasons their scope does not

admit of facts which lie outside the field of human observation. But the Gospels are not our only authorities for the Life of our Lord, if we use the phrase in the larger sense as including the life which the Church believes Him to be now living with God.

3. Circumstances have led our age to concentrate its studies upon the earthly life of Jesus Christ, and a great revival of interest in the records of that life is among the best signs of the time. But we pay too great a price for the enthusiasm which has been awakened by the reconstructed portrait of the historical Jesus, if our attention is diverted by it from the glorified Christ to whom witness is borne in the later books of the New Testament. Since the Day of Pentecost the Church has seen and heard greater things than even those which are related in the Synoptic Gospels, as the Fourth Gospel, with its fuller insight into the mystery of Christ, plainly hints.[1] If kings and righteous men desired to see the things which the Twelve saw and to hear what they heard, yet the experiences of the ministry have been surpassed by the revelations of the Spirit. *Even though we have known Christ after the flesh, yet now we know Him no more.*[2] S. Paul was in no danger of undervaluing the importance of the historical basis of Christianity; the gospel which he preached at Corinth was the gospel of the Cross and the Resurrection.[3] But the Christ he knew was not a man whose life was ended by the Cross and whose claim to pre-eminence rested only on a unique life and the ineffaceable marks of his influence on human thought and conduct. The Christ of the Epistles is a living Person who exists in the fulness of human nature behind the veil of sense, and is actively engaged in the shaping of events and the

---

[1] Cf. Jo. i. 50 f., xiv. 12, xvi. 14, 25 f.   [2] 2 Cor. v. 16.
[3] 1 Cor. xv. 1 ff..

salvation of men. The historical Christ has from the Apostle's point of view passed into the mystical, and the works and teaching of the ministry are surpassed, almost eclipsed, by the wonders of the life with God. If this thought lies in the background of the Apostle's difficult saying, it represents a position which to a less balanced mind might easily become hazardous. But it calls attention sharply and usefully to the supreme importance of the glorified life of our Lord, which an exclusive study of the earthly life may tempt us to neglect.

4. The purpose of these pages is to follow our Lord so far as we may into this higher life of the Spirit. In this attempt there will be no need to resort to speculation. If the Gospels fail us here, their place is taken by the Acts, the Epistles, and the Apocalypse, which contain the testimony of the Spirit of Jesus to the Ascended Christ. The Spirit of Jesus is the Spirit of Truth, and we are assured that in the Apostolic writings we are face to face with realities. What we are taught in the Epistles as to the glories of our Lord's life in heaven is no less matter of fact than the most certain features of the tradition preserved by the Synoptics. But the former are facts of another order, of which men on earth have no experience; and they could only be conveyed to the minds of the writers or made intelligible to their readers through symbolical language. Symbolism has been well-defined as 'indirect description,' 'description or expression by a system of equivalents';[1] and the symbolism of Scripture conveys to us the transcendent in terms of the phenomenal, and the higher things of the Spirit in terms of our own spiritual experience. For the time the symbol is our nearest approach to the reality, when heavenly things are presented to our minds; however

[1] Sanday, *Life of Christ in Recent Research*, p. 3.

much we may endeavour to 'dematerialize' symbols and get to the naked facts which lie behind them, as, for instance, by substituting modern philosophical terms for the Biblical words, we do little more than substitute one set of symbols for another; the ultimate truths remain impenetrable while we are here.[1] With symbols, then, we must be content in this high region of Christian faith. Yet the symbolical need not be fanciful, and in the teaching of the Spirit we are assured that it is not so; here it presents to us certainties as substantial as the physical or historical facts which can be described directly in the terms of common experience. The reader of these pages, then, is asked not to suffer the symbolism in which the New Testament doctrine of the ascended life of our Lord is draped to interfere with his sense of the actuality of the things that it represents.

5. Though the heavenly life of our Lord does not admit of historical treatment or of being presented to our thought in any but an indirect or symbolical method, our materials for forming a conception of its scope and purpose are abundant, and indeed not less ample than those which we possess for the study of His life on earth. Few persons who examine the second half of the New Testament with the purpose of collecting all that it teaches upon this subject will rise from the task without surprise at the wealth and variety of these revelations. It is certainly not through any want of Apostolic guidance if the glorified life of our Lord fills a relatively small place in modern preaching and thought.

The Creeds of Christendom, it may be said, do not encourage thought in this direction. They are content to confess that Jesus Christ has ascended to heaven and is on the right hand of God; of the life He lives there or the work with which He is occupied they have nothing to say.

---

[1] See G. Tyrrell, *Christianity at the Cross-roads*, p. 103.

INTRODUCTION. xv

But the Creeds are equally silent as to the contents of His earthly life, going straight from *natus* to *passus*, from ἐνανθρωπήσαντα to σταυρωθέντα, without a hint of the momentous events that intervened.[1] In both cases the omission is doubtless deliberate. The Creeds are not summaries of Christian doctrine, but bare *credenda*, consisting of the fundamental facts of Christianity; the filling up of the framework is left to the judgement of the Christian teacher, or to the study and reflexion of the individual believer.

6. The doctrine of the Ascended Life is among the spiritual things of the Christian Faith which cannot be received or assimilated unless the Spirit Himself interprets them to the inner man. Where there is no interior sympathy with the spiritual order, this whole side of Apostolic teaching, as S. Paul frankly confesses, cannot but incur the charge of 'foolishness,'[2] even though it may be received in respectful silence or find a conventional recognition. A study of the Heavenly Life calls for some uplifting of the heart to the Ascended Christ, some union with Him through the indwelling of His Spirit, or at the least some seeking of the things that are above, where He is seated on the right hand of God. In proportion as we thus ascend in heart and mind the Exalted Manhood becomes to us a present reality, and its great functions and energies stand out before our eyes with ever-growing distinctness, till the whole glorious vision takes its place among the deepest convictions and the most powerful motives of our lives.

---

[1] The words καὶ ἐν ἀνθρώποις πολιτευσάμενον, which Eusebius of Caesarea (Socr. *H.E.* i. 8), quotes in his appeal to the ancient creed of his own Church, stand alone as a reference to the Lord's life in Palestine. See Dean Stanley's remark upon them in *Eastern Church*, p. 157.

[2] 1 Cor. ii. 14.

ὁ καθήμενος ἐν δεξιᾷ τοῦ πατρός,
ἐλέησον ἡμᾶς.

I.

THE ASCENSION AND THE SESSION.

TWO steps brought the risen Lord to the full glory of His life with God. He *was received up into heaven*, and there He *sat down at the right hand of God*.[1]

The two great creeds of the Western Church confess the Ascension and Session in almost identical words: 'He ascended into heaven, and sitteth on the right hand of [God] the Father [Almighty].'[2] Their witness goes further back than the existing forms, for the Apostles' Creed rests on the Roman baptismal creed of the second century, and the 'Nicene,' *i.e.* the Constantinopolitan, Creed reflects the early creed of the Church of Jerusalem. Belief in the Ascension and Session was universal in the early Church, both in East and West. 'The Church,' writes Irenaeus,[3] 'though scattered through-

[1] 'Mc.' xvi. 19.
[2] 'Ascendit ad caelos, sedit ad dexteram dei patris omnipotentis.' Ἀνελθόντα εἰς τοὺς οὐρανούς, καὶ καθεζόμενον ἐκ δεξιῶν τοῦ πατρός.
[3] *C. haer.* I. 9. 5.

out the whole world to the ends of the earth, has received from the Apostles and their disciples her faith... in One Christ Jesus... and His assumption in the flesh[1] into the heavens.' 'The rule of faith,' says Tertullian,[2] 'teaches us to believe that... Jesus Christ... was carried up into heaven and sat at the right hand of the Father.' Sometimes the Ascension only is mentioned, sometimes the Session; but either suggests the other, and the great majority of ancient creed-forms expressly acknowledge both.

The same belief meets us when we go back to the writings of the Apostolic age. The Synoptic Gospels indeed, if we except the appendix to S. Mark, are nearly silent[3] on the subject, probably because, as Dr. Hort pointed out, 'the Ascension did not lie within the proper scope of the Gospels... its true place was at the head of the Acts of the Apostles, as the preparation for the Day of Pentecost, and thus the beginning of the history of the Church.' There, accordingly, we find a full account of the event; the writer of Acts, whose 'former treatise' had recorded the acts and teaching of the Lord *until the day in which he was received up* (ἀνελήμφθη), relates how after a last instruction to the Eleven,

[1] τὴν ἔνσαρκον ἀνάληψιν.

[2] *De praescr.* 13: 'In caelos ereptum sedisse ad dexteram patris.'

[3] Lc. xxiv. 51, if we accept the Westcott-Hort theory of 'Western non-interpolations,' has only διέστη ἀπ' αὐτῶν (*Notes on Select Readings*, p. 73).

THE ASCENSION AND THE SESSION

as they were looking he was taken up (ἐπήρθη), *and a cloud received him out of their sight. Ye beheld him going* (πορευόμενον) *into heaven*, is the interpretation put upon His ascent by a vision of angels which presently appeared.[1] Under the teaching of the Spirit the event assumed a further significance. Jesus had been *by the right hand of God exalted*; the Psalm had been fulfilled which said, *Sit thou on my right hand. The heavens must receive* Him *until the times of restoration of all things*.[2] In the heavens, accordingly, Stephen saw Him *standing on the right hand of God*; out of heaven the light of the persecuted Lord fell on the persecutor Saul.[3] The Epistles assume the Ascension as they assume the Resurrection; facts so familiar to the new Churches are not often expressly rehearsed in the brief letters which deal with the many pressing problems of the first age. Yet there is ample evidence that the Ascension and Session were not overlooked by any of the great writers of the second half of the New Testament. *Jesus Christ*, S. Peter writes, *is on the right hand of God, having gone into heaven.*[4] *It is Christ Jesus*, says S. Paul, *that died, yea rather, that was raised from the dead; who is at the right hand of God. God raised him from the dead, and made him to sit at his right*

---

[1] Acts i. 2, 9, 11.　　[2] Acts ii. 33 f., iii. 21.
[3] Acts vii. 55 f., ix. 3, xxii. 6, xxvi. 12.　　[4] 1 Peter iii. 22.

hand in the heavenlies (ἐν τοῖς ἐπουρανίοις). *He that descended is the same also that ascended far above all the heavens. God highly exalted him.* He was *received up in glory.*[1] The Epistle to the Hebrews, which is occupied with the heavenly life of the Lord, rests on the historical fact of the Ascension, which it enunciates many times.[2] The life and work of the Ascended Christ are its chief themes. He is *a great high priest who has passed through the heavens. We have such a high priest, who sat down on the right hand of the throne of the Majesty in the heavens.* He *entered in once for all into the holy place ... into heaven itself, now to appear before the face of God for us.* He *sat down on the right hand of God.* The Johannine writings are not less explicit. Though the fourth Gospel does not embrace the Ascension, it presupposes the fact again and again:[3] *What if ye should behold the Son of Man ascending where he was before? I go unto him that sent me; I go to the Father and ye behold me no more. I am no more in the world ... I come to thee. I ascend unto my Father and your Father, and my God and your God.* The first Epistle echoes these sayings of the Gospel when it says that *we have an Advocate with the Father* (πρὸς τὸν πατέρα);[4] and

---

[1] Rom. viii. 34; Eph. i. 20, iv. 10; Phil. ii. 9; 1 Tim. iii. 6.
[2] Heb. iv. 14, viii. 1, ix. 12, 24, x. 12, xii. 2.
[3] Jo. vi. 62, xvi. 5, 10, xvii. 11, xx. 17.
[4] 1 Jo. ii. 1.

THE ASCENSION AND THE SESSION 5

the Apocalypse, like the Epistle to the Hebrews, owes its *motif* to the Ascension and Session, which are presupposed in every page of the book.

What conception of these events may be gained from references made to them in the New Testament?

1. *The Ascension.* From one point of view the Ascension was the last parting of the risen Lord from His disciples. He *parted from them* when He ascended, as He had parted from them at the end of each of His appearances after the Resurrection. But whereas the previous partings had been instantaneous, through the sudden vanishing of the human form,[1] this was *as they were looking*;[2] the process could be observed up to a certain point; and whereas the other separations were for a few hours or days, this was final and beyond recall. It was followed by no fresh appearances, or by none of the same kind—none which placed the Lord evidently in their midst, or brought them into such contact with Him that He could be handled by them, and on one occasion even ate and drank in their presence.[3] The Ascension put an end to all intercourse of this nature: it was a departing from the world, a withdrawal once for all

---

[1] Lc. xxiv. 31 ἄφαντος ἐγένετο ἀπ' αὐτῶν.
[2] Acts i. 9 f. βλεπόντων αὐτῶν ... ὡς ἀτενίζοντες ἦσαν.
[3] Lc. xxiv. 42, Acts x. 41.

from the whole order under which men live on this side of the grave. It completed the alienation from the things of sense which the Resurrection began.[1]

But the manner of this final departure—the lifting up of the human form from the earth, and the apparent passing upwards of the cloud which received it out of sight—suggested a further aspect of the event. Jesus left the world because the time had come for Him to go to the Father. His departure was a 'going up,' as His entrance into the world had been a 'coming down.' He who had descended now ascended where He was before.[2]

'Ascended' in our English creed has come from the *ascendit* of the Latin, apparently by way of the Prymer of 1538 and the *Necessary Doctrine* of 1543.[3] In the English New Testament 'ascend' seems to appear first in Tyndale's version of 1534 as the equivalent of ἀναβαίνειν. But ἀναβαίνειν, *ascendere*, is not the only word used by the New Testament writers in connexion with the Ascension of our Lord; another and slightly more frequent term is ἀναλαμβάνεσθαι, *adsumi*.[4] The 'going up'

---

[1] Cf. Jo. xx. 17 οὔπω ἀναβέβηκα πρὸς τὸν πατέρα.

[2] Jo. vi. 41, 51 ὁ καταβάς. *Ib.* 62. Cf. Eph. iv. 10 ὁ καταβὰς αὐτός ἐστιν καὶ ὁ ἀναβάς.

[3] Earlier English versions of the *Credo* had for *ascendit*, *astah* or *steih* (*steich*, *stiged*, *steig*, *steyed*); see Heurtley, *Creeds of the Western Church*, pp. 87-99.

[4] Ἀναβαίνειν occurs in this reference, Jo. vi. 62, xx. 17; Eph. iv. 8 f.; ἀναλαμβάνεσθαι, 'Mc.' xvi. 19; Acts i. 2, 11, 22; 1 Tim. iii. 16.

THE ASCENSION AND THE SESSION

of the Son of Man into heaven was also His 'being taken up,' the Ascension was an Assumption; and the words answer to two complementary aspects of the event. The one represents Jesus Christ as entering the Presence of the Father of His own will and right; the other lays the emphasis on the Father's act by which He was exalted as the reward of His obedience unto death. Both words had been prepared for the use of the Gospel by their employment in the Greek Old Testament. *Who shall ascend* (LXX ἀναβήσεται) *into the hill of the Lord?* the Psalmist asks, and answers himself, *He that hath clean hands and a pure heart.*[1] Elijah, we read, *was taken up*[2] (LXX ἀνελήμφθη) *in a whirlwind into heaven.*[3] Both passages are appropriately used by the Church on Ascension Day; our Lord is at once the Sinless Man who was able to ascend into the celestial city and stand in the holy place, and the great Prophet of Israel who, His work accomplished, was taken up to His place on high.

The Lord 'went up,' or 'was taken up,' into heaven. Both our creeds in the original have the plural 'into the heavens.'[4] It is amply justified by S. Paul's words, *He that ascended far above all*

---

[1] Ps. xxiv. (xxiii.) 3.   [2] 2 Kings ii. 11.

[3] The Heb. has simply וַיַּעַל, 'went up;' but cf. ii. 1 בְּהַעֲלוֹת (LXX ἐν τῷ ἀνάγειν). In reference to Enoch the LXX (Gen. v. 24) uses μετέθηκεν (לָקַח); cf. Heb. xi. 5.

[4] 'In caelos,' εἰς τοὺς οὐρανούς.

the heavens,[1] and by those of the writer of Hebrews: *passed through the heavens, ... made higher than the heavens*.[2] On the other hand, in our only full account of the Ascension Jesus Christ is described simply as *going into heaven* (εἰς τὸν οὐρανόν).[3] The difference is perhaps not without significance; as seen by the spectators, the ascent was bounded by the sky, but viewed in the light of the Spirit, it carried the Lord beyond all the bounds of space. A conception which limits His ascent to any region however remote from the earth, or locates His ascended life in any part of the material universe, falls vastly short of the primitive belief; no third heaven, no seventh heaven of Jewish speculation, no central sun of later conjecture, meets the requirements of an exaltation to the Throne of God. As the Incarnation was not a physical descent, so the return of the Incarnate to the Father was not a physical elevation;[4] the momentary lifting up of the risen Christ in the sight of the Eleven can only be regarded as a symbol of the lifting up of our humanity in Him to that spiritual order which is as far above our present life as the visible heaven is above the earth. It is true that our Lord returned to the Father not as he came, but for

---

[1] Eph. iv. 10.   [2] Heb. iv. 14, vii. 26.   [3] Acts i. 11.

[4] 'We are not to think of this Ascension of Christ as of a change of position ... it is rather a change of the mode of existence' (Westcott, *Historic Faith*, p. 80).

THE ASCENSION AND THE SESSION

ever united with human nature, the Word made Flesh. But the Resurrection had placed the Flesh of the Word so far under the control of the Spirit that His body, as the Gospels shew, was, even before the Ascension, independent, when He so willed, of the laws that govern matter.[1] In the glorified Body, as we must suppose, the contrast is complete; and while the Sacred Humanity retains all that is essential to human nature, it must needs be free from all the conditions of space. Our Lord indeed likens His Ascension to a journey to a far country;[2] the distance between the human life of even the great Son of Man upon earth and the perfect life of God is immeasurable. But it is not such a distance as can be crossed by any physical movement, nor was the journey by which it was covered one that needed days or hours or even minutes to accomplish. The cloud which seemed to mark the Lord's upward way lingered in sight perhaps for long, and the Eleven, from their place upon the hillside, watched it gradually disappear. But the Lord's journey was surely completed in the momentary act of will by which He finally left the world, and went to the Father; that instant all the glory of God shone about Him, and He was in heaven. The sight was not altogether new to Him; in the depth of His Divine consciousness the Son of Man had

---

[1] Cf. Gore, *Body of Christ*, p. 128 ff.
[2] Lc. xix. 12 ἐπορεύθη εἰς χώραν μακράν.

memories of the glory which in His pre-incarnate life he had had *with the Father before the world was.*[1] But the human soul of Christ up to the moment of the Ascension had had no experience of the full vision of God which burst upon it when He was taken up. This was the goal of His human life, the joy set before His human soul; and in the moment of the Ascension it was attained.

2. *The Session.* 'He ascended... and sitteth'— so say the Apostles' and 'Nicene' Creeds; 'He ascended... He sat down' is the reading of the best text of the *Quicumque*.[2] Both present and past can claim support from the New Testament,[3] and it is obvious that they are not inconsistent; the Session, which began at the Ascension, continues to the present hour.

All references to the Session of the Ascended Christ rest ultimately on the 110th Psalm, *The Lord saith unto my lord, Sit thou at my right hand, until I make thine enemies thy footstool.* That our Lord had this Psalm in mind during the last week of His life and applied it to Himself as Messiah is clear from the questions

---

[1] Jo. xvii. 5: cf. the remarkable words of Jo. iii. 13, where, however, ὁ ὢν ἐν τῷ οὐρανῷ is probably an insertion; see Westcott's Additional Note.

[2] *Ascendit... sedet*; ἀνελθόντα καὶ καθεζόμενον. On the *Quicumque* text see C. H. Turner, in *J.T.S.* xi. p. 410.

[3] For *sitteth*, see Mc. xiv. 62, Col. iii. 1, 1 Pet. iii. 22; for '*sat*,' 'Mc.' xvi. 19, Eph. i. 21, Heb. i. 3, viii. 1, xii. 2 (κεκάθικεν).

which He put to the Temple crowd on the Tuesday of Holy Week; nor can it be doubted that He referred to it again when in the grey dawn of Good Friday He warned the High Priest and Sanhedrin, *Ye shall see the Son of Man sitting at the right hand of power.*[1] That this Psalm found its fulfilment at the Ascension was the fixed belief of the Apostolic age, as we see from its use by S. Peter on the Day of Pentecost, and the indirect reference to it in nearly a dozen other passages of the Acts, Epistles and Apocalypse.[2]

To the 110th Psalm, then, we must look for a clue to the interpretation of the phrase. A king is addressed,[3] who is made by Divine decree assessor of Jahveh, and is seated at His right hand until such time as all his enemies have been subjugated. The same person is also appointed to be permanently priest after the archetype of the priest-king Melchizedek. Is the Psalmist a writer of the Maccabean age who has in view Jonathan, or perhaps Simon the successor of Jonathan, of whom we read in 1 Maccabees that *the Jews and the priests were*

[1] Mc. xii. 36, xiv. 62. In the latter place the imagery is partly drawn from Dan. vii. 11, but ἐκ δεξιῶν καθεζόμενον is clearly from Psalm cx.

[2] Acts ii. 33 ff.: cf. Acts vii. 55 f., Rom. viii. 34, Eph. i. 20, Col. iii. 1, Heb. i. 3, 13, viii. 1, x. 12, xii. 2, 1 Pet. iii. 22, Apoc. iii. 21, xii. 5.

[3] For an exposition of the Psalm see Dr. Driver in the *Expositor* for March, 1910, and for another study Dr. Emery Barnes in *Lex in corde*.

well pleased that he should be their leader and high priest for ever?[1] Or is the Priest-King of the Psalms simply an idealizing picture of the theocratic King, drawn by a late Psalmist who had caught the inspiration of the Messianic hope? In any case the general purpose of the writer is clear. The ideal King is seen seated on the right of Jahveh Himself, or next in honour to Him;[2] he is assured of complete victory over his enemies, on whose necks he will one day, after the manner of victorious captains, place his feet.[3]

The use of this Psalm in the New Testament in reference to the Session of Our Lord at the right hand of God invites us to contemplate Him as invested with the highest honour of which humanity is capable, recognized as the Father's Viceroy, and assured of final victory over all who oppose His rule. *We behold him ... crowned with glory and honour ... from henceforth expecting till his enemies be made his footstool.*[4] The Son of Man has heard the oracle, *Sit thou at my right hand,* and has taken His seat on the Father's throne. It is not difficult here to distinguish symbol from fact. The Throne, the Right Hand, the act of sitting down, the posture of

---

[1] 1 Macc. xiv. 41. For the difficulties presented by this view, see Kirkpatrick, *Psalms*, p. 664; Driver, *l.c.*

[2] See the remarkable illustration in 1 Macc. x. 63.

[3] Cf. Josh. x. 24, 1 Kings v. 3. [4] Heb. ii. 9, x. 13.

THE ASCENSION AND THE SESSION 13

the seated King, are as clearly symbolical as the final placing of the Lord's enemies under His feet. But the exaltation and glorification of the Sacred Manhood of our Lord, the exercise by Him of all authority in heaven and on earth, the certainty of His final triumph over sin and death, are facts, and the most potent facts in the life of the human race.

Other thoughts to which neither the Psalmist nor his Apostolic interpreters point may be suggested by the seated posture of the Ascended Christ. 'The notion of sitting (so writes Bishop Pearson) implieth rest, quietness, and indisturbance... Christ is ascended into heaven, where resting from all pains and sorrows He is seated free from all disturbance and opposition.'[1] The weariness of the ministry and the sufferings of the Cross were for ever at an end when he sat down at the right hand of God. As after the creation God is said to have *rested on the seventh day from all his work which he had made*, so, it may be conceived, the Incarnate Son rests now with God from the work of His mission to the world. But this analogy does not present itself to the mind of the author of Hebrews, when he discourses on the sabbath rest of the Creator in close connexion with the Ascension of our Lord. Nor is it more than superficial, for the rest of the Creator was merely

---

[1] Similarly Bishop Westcott, *Historic Faith*, p. 52: 'the image of Christ's Session is that of perfect rest.'

a ceasing to create; weariness and pain have no place in the life of unincarnate Godhead. If the Incarnate Son kept sabbath after the Cross, it was during His brief abode in Hades that He did so, when His flesh rested in hope of the Resurrection.[1] It seems precarious, then, to connect the idea of repose with our Lord's Session in heaven. Victory is no doubt represented by it: *he that overcometh*, the Spirit says to the Churches, *I will give to him to sit down with me in my throne, as I also overcame, and sat down with my Father in his throne.*[2] But our Lord's victory over the world in the days of His flesh was but an earnest of the longer warfare and the more complete conquest which are the work of His ascended life. When He sat down at the right hand of power, it was not for a brief cessation from warfare, but for an age-long conflict with the powers of evil. 'Sitting' is not always the posture of rest. Some of the hardest work of life is done by the monarch seated in his cabinet, and the statesman at his desk; and the seated Christ, like the four living creatures round about Him, rests not day nor night from the unintermitting energies of heaven.

When the Apostolic Church thought of the ascended Lord as seated in heaven, she had in her

---

[1] Ps. xvi. 9. But neither the Heb. (יִשְׁכֹּן) nor the LXX (κατασκηνώσει) suggests a reference to the sabbath.

[2] Apoc. iii. 21.

hands a corrective to the tendency to expect His immediate return. The Psalm which painted the figure of the Seated Christ might well have warned her that the end was not yet; further, the words '*Sit ... until*,' while limiting the Session to a period of time, suggest that the period will not be brief. Stephen, indeed, saw the Son of Man in heaven standing, as if ready to go forth at a moment's notice; and such a picture might well have been drawn in view of His ignorance of the time of His Coming.[1] But the Psalmist's description dominated Christian thought in the Apostolic age, and through the influence of the first age has moulded the creed of Christendom; and certainly it agrees better with the facts of history. As the interval between the Ascension and the Return lengthens century by century, the Church takes heart when she remembers the Seated Figure of the expectant Christ. He waits, seated on the Throne; we wait with Him, busy with our watch and our service on earth.

[1] Mc. xiii. 32 οὐδὲ ὁ υἱός.

II.

THE KING.

THE Ascension was the coronation of the Christ, and the Session His enthronement. *Crowned with glory and honour*,[1] He sat down with His Father in the Father's throne.[2] There *he must reign till* the Father has *put all enemies under his feet*.[3]

In the Synoptic Gospels Jesus is the King's Son[4] rather than the King; once, indeed, He assumes the royal title, but with reference to the final scene in the world's history, when before the eyes of the world the Son of Man *shall sit on the throne of his glory*. The postponement is the more remarkable, since kingship was a chief feature in the portrait of Messiah as it is drawn both in the Old Testament and in post-canonical Jewish writings. His prototype is David or Solomon, the anointed King of Israel. When in the second Psalm *the kings of the earth set themselves against Jahveh and against his*

[1] Heb. ii. 9.   [2] Apoc. iii. 21.
[3] 1 Cor. xv. 25.   [4] Mt. xxii. 2; cf. xxv. 34.

THE KING

Anointed, the answer comes, *Yet I have set my King upon my holy hill of Zion.*[1] Isaiah foretells, *Behold a king shall reign in righteousness*;[2] Ezekiel, *My servant David* shall be *prince among them* and *king over them*;[3] Zechariah, *Behold, thy king, cometh unto thee.*[4] The Messianic hope of the last half century before Christ was the hope of a King, and the Psalms of Solomon see in the coming reign of Messiah the salvation of Israel: [5] *raise up unto them their King, the son of David...and there shall be no iniquity in his days in their midst, for all shall be holy, and their King is the Lord Messiah.*[6] The charge laid against Jesus before the procurator was that, acting on these expectations, He had made Himself a king, and thus posed as a rival of Caesar.[7] As a matter of fact He had withdrawn from the multitudes when they would have forced Him into that false position.[8] Yet before Pilate He did not deny His kingly character, only affirming, *My kingdom is not of this world*, or *not from hence.*[9] The title on the Cross, therefore, though inexact, was not radically untrue; a king lay dying there, though not one who was in any exclusive or earthly

---

[1] Ps. ii. 2, 6.   [2] Isa. xxxii. 1.   [3] Ezek. xxxiv. 24, xxxvi. 24.
[4] Zech. ix. 9.   [5] Ps. Sol. xvii. 23, 36.
[6] So the Greek, κύριος χριστός; Heb. probably מְשִׁיחַ יְהוָה, the Lord's Anointed. See Ryle and James *ad loc.*
[7] Lc. xxii. 2, Jo. xix. 12.   [8] Jo. vi. 15.   [9] Jo. xviii. 36.

sense *the King of the Jews.* The penitent robber came nearer to the truth when he said, *Jesus, remember me, when thou comest in thy kingdom.*[1] It was borne in upon his mind that in some mysterious way the kingdom was to be reached through the Cross, and lay beyond it; and his words almost echo the Lord's description of Himself as about to go *into a far country, to receive for himself a Kingdom and to return.*[2]

The Kingdom was received at the Ascension, the far journey which carried Jesus from earth to heaven. This was at once realized by the Apostles, so soon as they came under the teaching of the Spirit. Their Master, they openly preached, was David's son, raised up *to sit upon his throne.*[3] Or, with fuller insight into the nature of the Kingdom, they taught that God had exalted Him to be *a Prince and a Saviour, for to give repentance to Israel and remission of sins.*[4] When it became clear that these gifts were not restricted to Israel, the missionaries of the Gospel carried to the Gentiles the doctrine of the Christ-King. At Thessalonica the old charge of disloyalty towards Caesar was brought against S. Paul's disciples: *these all act contrary to the decrees of Caesar, saying that there is another king, one Jesus.*[5] It may have been through fear of exciting the suspicions of

[1] Lc. xxiii. 42. [2] Lc. xix. 12. [3] Acts ii. 30.
[4] Acts v. 31. [5] Acts xvii. 7.

THE KING

the heathen that S. Paul henceforth abstained from applying the title of 'King' or 'Emperor' ($\beta\alpha\sigma\iota\lambda\epsilon\acute{u}s$) to the ascended Christ; certainly the equivalent term 'Lord' ($\kappa\acute{u}\rho\iota os$) seems to be everywhere preferred in his Epistles, and the short creed of the first generation of believers ran 'Jesus is Lord,'[1] and not, as it well might have run, 'Jesus is King.' The Empire had hitherto shewn no hostility to the Church, and was still restraining the forces of evil which the Apostle foresaw would quickly gather if it were *taken out of the way.*[2] It would have been impolitic to hasten the catastrophe by the use of language which would evidently give offence, and S. Paul refrained accordingly. But before the Apocalypse was written, the position of affairs had changed : the Empire was already openly antichristian; Rome under Nero had already drunk the blood of the saints, and Domitian seemed on the point to repeat the atrocities of his predecessor; in Asia, at all events, there was a prospect of immediate and ruthless persecution.[3] Moreover, the cult of Caesar had now assumed the character of a heathen Messianism; the alternative, 'Christ or Caesar,' could no longer have been avoided had Domitian lived and the Caesar-priests carried out their plans.[4] In S. John's belief,

---

[1] 1 Cor. xii. 3 εἰπεῖν Κύριος Ἰησοῦς.   [2] 2 Th. ii. 7.
[3] Apoc. ii. 10, iii. 10, xii. 13, xiii. 7, etc.
[4] Apoc. xiii. 17, xiv. 9, xix. 19.

then, the time had come to accept the challenge, and to proclaim the Empire of Jesus Christ. This is done by the Seer of the Apocalypse without reserve. The Ascended Christ is *Ruler of the kings of the earth*; He is *King of kings, and Lord of lords*; His elect shall reign *with Christ a thousand years*.[1] A great voice in heaven is heard to say, *Now is come the Kingdom of our God, and the authority of his Christ*; another voice cries, *The Kingdom of the world is become the Kingdom of our Lord and of his Christ*.[2] With Domitian at Rome claiming to be called 'our Lord and God,'[3] there could no longer be any hesitation on the part of the Church as to the duty of proclaiming the Ascended Christ as the Overlord of the Emperor, the true Ruler of the world and Viceroy of God.

Were these magnificent titles mere echoes of the Jewish Messianic Hope, or empty claims flung in the face of the Roman persecutor by men who had been driven to desperation by his cruelty? Or, do they correspond to actual functions which the Seer knew to have been committed to the Ascended Christ? And if so, what are these functions, and how are they discharged? The New Testament supplies the answer.

We begin with the words of the risen Christ, spoken, it seems, as the forty days were approaching

---

[1] Apoc. i. 5, xix. 16, xx. 4.   [2] Apoc. xi. 15, xii. 10.
[3] Sueton. *Domitian*, 13: 'dominus et deus noster hoc fieri iubet.'

an end. *All authority was given* (ἐδόθη) *unto me in heaven and on earth.*[1] The past tense carries our thoughts back to the pre-incarnate life of the Son and the eternal purpose of the Father. The grant was made before time began.[2] But it was conditioned by the acts in time of the Incarnate Son —the long obedience which culminated in the Sacrifice of the Cross: the change which began with the Resurrection and was completed by the Ascension. Then at length the Father's gift was realized in full; the authority of the Christ over all created persons and things, visible and invisible, became an accomplished fact.

It was 'authority' (ἐξουσία) which the Father granted and the Son received: the right to act accompanied by the requisite power. Authority was no new claim on the part of our Lord. He had asserted it at the outset of His ministry: *the Son of Man hath authority on earth to forgive sins.*[3] The same note was heard in all His teaching, and seen in all His works.[4] Moreover, He claimed the right to delegate His authority, and did so both before and after the

---

[1] Mt. xxviii. 18. Dan. vii. 14 was perhaps in the Lord's mind: *there was given him dominion* (LXX ἐξουσία) *and glory and a kingdom, that all the peoples, nations, and languages should serve him; his dominion* (LXX and Th. ἡ ἐξουσία αὐτοῦ) *is an everlasting dominion.*

[2] Cf. Mt. xi. 27 πάντα μοι παρεδόθη παρὰ τοῦ πατρός μου, and see W. C. Allen *ad loc.*

[3] Mc. ii. 10.   [4] Mt. vii. 29, Mc. i. 27.

Resurrection.[1] Even before the Passion He was conscious that, for the purposes of His mission, His authority extended *over all flesh.*[2] What was new in the final assertion of this claim which He made on the eve of the Ascension was the inclusion of the whole creation within the scope of His power. All previous claims of authority to speak in the Father's Name, to remit sins, to expel the forces of evil, to give eternal life to all whom the Father had given Him, fall vastly short of one which covers both earth and heaven.

1. *All authority in heaven.* How is this tremendous phrase to be interpreted? We may begin with a great text from S. Paul where this side of the Lord's present exaltation comes under review. God, we read, made Christ *to sit at his right hand in the heavenlies* (ἐν τοῖς ἐπουρανίοις), *far above all rule and authority and power and dominion, and every name that is named, not only in this world, but also in that which is to come.*[3] Here, as elsewhere, the Apostle assumes the existence of a graded hierarchy in the heavenly world, corresponding to the successive grades of official life at an earthly court. But far above all these he sees Jesus Christ, invested with a dignity which has no parallel even in the court of heaven. S. Peter has the same conception: Jesus Christ *is on the right hand of God... angels and*

[1] Mc. vi. 7, Jo. xx. 21 f.   [2] Jo. xvii. 2.   [3] Eph. i. 20 f.

authorities and powers being made subject unto him.[1] So also the author of Hebrews : He has *become by so much superior to the angels, as he hath inherited a more excellent name than they.* They are *ministering spirits,* He is the Incarnate Son ; the name of Son belongs to Him by inheritance, and by the Ascension He has come into His own.[2] The other heavenly authorities recognize this and do Him homage: it was the purpose of the Father that *in the name of Jesus every knee should bow, of things in heaven* (ἐπουρανίων)..., *and that every tongue should confess that Jesus Christ is Lord, to the glory of God the Father.*[3] We see the King's Son, invested with the King's authority, passing through the ranks of the great nobles of the heavenly order ; and, as He passes, every one of these spiritual powers does obeisance, while from the whole assembly there rises the creed of the primitive Church, *Jesus is Lord.* S. John's ears are opened to hear the hymn of praise that follows : *I heard a voice of many angels round about the throne ... and the number of them was ten thousand times ten thousand ... saying with a great voice, Worthy is the Lamb that hath been slain to receive the power and riches and wisdom and might and honour and glory and blessing.*[4]

[1] 1 Pet. iii. 22.
[2] Heb. i. 4. Cf. Westcott *ad loc.*: 'Probably not the name of "Son," simply ... but the Name in which was gathered up all that Christ was found to be by believers.'
[3] Phil. ii. 9 ff. [4] Apoc. v. 11 f.

In the two moments of the Lord's deepest humiliation angels ministered to Him, and they would, had He so willed, have hastened in their legions to save Him from the Cross.[1] So, since His exaltation, they 'alway do Him service in heaven,' even as they serve the Father whose authority He wields. *Made a little lower than the angels, seen of angels* in His agony,[2] He now receives their worship; they are His, and they do His will.[3] Nothing is done in that great unknown world, which we commonly call 'heaven,' without His initiating, guiding, determining authority. Processes inconceivable by our minds are being carried forward beyond the veil by agencies equally inconceivable. It is enough for the Church to know that all which is being done there is done by the authority of her Lord.

Yet, if 'heaven' be used in the wider sense of 'the spiritual world,' S. Paul does not hide from us that there are intelligences in it which not only refuse to submit to the rule of the Christ, but actively resist it. He saw them at work in the great struggle which had already begun between the Church and the World. *Our wrestling is not against flesh and blood, but against the principalities, against the powers, against the world-rulers of this darkness, against the spiritual hosts of wickedness in the heavenly places.*[4] The darkness of the heathen world was under the control of

---

[1] Mc. i. 13, Lc. xxii. 43, Mt. xxvi. 53. [2] Heb. ii. 7, 1 Tim. iii. 16.
[3] Mt. xiii. 41. [4] Eph. vi. 12.

THE KING

rulers stronger than the Proconsul or the Emperor. There was a hierarchy of evil as well as of good, immaterial and unseen, forces which had at their command all the worst passions of men; and these were all leagued against the Kingdom of Christ on earth. S. John in Patmos saw the struggle begin in the spiritual world itself: *there was war in heaven*: the archangel *Michael* (*the great prince* who, according to Daniel, stands for the children of the holy people)[1] *and his angels going forth to war with the Dragon.* The Seer heard the din of principality clashing arms with principality, and power with power, and he saw Satan and his angels cast out of heaven to the earth and in the end out of the earth into the lake of fire.[2] Meanwhile the very air seemed to be infested by the evil spiritual force, which worked in the enemies of the Christ and sought to overwhelm His friends.[3] If such language is difficult for us to understand, who live in an age of dominant Christianity, it is to be remembered that our difficulty bears witness to the extent of the victory which has been gained over the forces of evil since the first century. The *spiritual hosts of wickedness*[4] are not yet under the feet of Christ, but they are fighting, as history shews, a losing battle.

---

[1] Dan. xii. 1.   [2] Apoc. xii. 7 ff., xx. 10.
[3] Eph. ii. 2 τὸν ἄρχοντα τῆς ἐξουσίας τοῦ ἀέρος, τοῦ πνεύματος τοῦ νῦν ἐνεργοῦντος ἐν τοῖς υἱοῖς τῆς ἀπειθίας.
[4] Eph. vi. 12.

2. But to leave the spiritual world, and turn to the phenomenal. *All authority*, the ascending Christ said, *was given to me ... on earth*. What is the meaning of this claim to exercise supreme control over visible nature and mankind?

No Christian, who follows the teaching of S. Paul and S. John, can doubt that the Eternal Word or Son is supreme in the Kingdom of Nature. *All things have been created through him and unto him, and he is before all things, and in him all things consist.*[1] *All things were made by him, and without him was made not even one single thing* (οὐδὲ ἕν). *That which hath been made was life in him* (ὃ γέγονεν ἐν αὐτῷ ζωὴ ἦν).[2] The two greatest teachers of the Apostolic age agree in representing the Son as not only the Agent of Creation, but its immanent vital force and its 'principle of cohesion,' the source of 'that unity and solidarity which makes it a cosmos instead of a chaos.'[3] He upholds, or rather, bears (φέρων), *all things by the word of his power*;[4] and the support He gives to the universe is not that of 'an Atlas sustaining the dead weight of the world,' but of a living immanent Power; and it includes movement, progress towards an end.

---

[1] Col. i. 16 f.
[2] Jo. i. 3 f. On the punctuation, see Westcott's Additional Note.
[3] Lightfoot on Col. i. 17.
[4] Heb. i. 3 (see Westcott *ad loc.*).

THE KING

Even in His earthly humiliation the Incarnate Word manifested unique power over Nature. No reasonable criticism can resolve all *the works which none other did*[1] into efforts of the imagination on the part of those who witnessed His ministry or of those who reported or recorded their testimony. Psychological considerations are certainly pressed too far when they are made to account for the supernatural element which pervades all the Gospels in almost every page. The personality of the Christ may suffice to explain the general impression of superhuman power which was left on the minds of the men who were associated with Him, but it fails to explain either the greater miracles which are described in detail, or the vast scale on which the unrecorded 'signs' were given. We feel ourselves to be in the presence of One who, unless the records are the wildest of romances, does by whatever means impress His will on the forces of Nature after a fashion which even in this age of physical discovery is impossible to ourselves. Plain men, as they read the Gospels, still ask themselves the question, *Whence hath this man these things ... what mean such mighty works wrought by his hands?*[2]

But if in the days of His flesh the Incarnate Son through the Spirit exercised powers over Nature such as no other man ever possessed, what limit

[1] Jo. xv. 24. [2] Mc. vi. 2.

shall be put to the authority of the glorified manhood? 'His ascension,' it has been well said, 'is the enlargement of His human capacities to a degree that we cannot measure, and it carries with it a corresponding increase of the content of His consciousness and of the exercise of His power.'[1] The Epistle to the Hebrews[2] has brought us to see in the Ascended Humanity a fulfilment of the glowing words in which the eighth Psalm describes the supremacy of man over the rest of creation: *thou madest him to have dominion over the works of thy hands; thou hast put all things under his feet: all sheep and oxen, yea, and the beasts of the field; the fowl of the air, and the fish of the sea.*[3] Modern knowledge has almost indefinitely extended the limits of this control, making man master of natural forces the very existence of which was unknown to the Biblical writers, or in some instances to the last generation; and it is not improbable that the coming years will witness an enormous enlargement of such human powers. But in Jesus Christ humanity has already entered upon the fulness of its inheritance: whatever can be done by a human nature which from the first was free from sin and has now been perfected in all its powers is within the reach of the glorified manhood of our Lord. How far such a nature may carry its control

---

[1] Bp. Weston, *The One Christ*, p. 290.   [2] Heb. ii. 5 ff.
[3] Ps. viii. 6 ff.

over the physical world we have no means of judging. Moreover, it is to be remembered that the glorified humanity is, so far as manhood can be this, a perfect medium for the self-expression of the Divine Word. The personal Force which lies behind the forces of Nature, carrying them on to the accomplishment of their destiny, works through the human mind and will of the Ascended Christ, so far as the human in its perfected state is able to respond to the Divine.

In Christ, then, Nature is already under the feet of Man. But what shall be said of Man's submission to the authority of Christ?

Another Psalm led the Apostolic Church to the true answer here. When for the first time the Apostles were threatened by the Sanhedrin, their thoughts turned to the familiar words, *The rulers take counsel together against Jahveh and against his Anointed.* But as they read on, there came the words of promise to the Christ, *Ask of me, and I will give thee the nations for thine inheritance, and the uttermost parts of the earth for thy possession; thou shalt break them with a rod of iron; thou shalt dash them in pieces like a potter's vessel.*[1] Christ, they knew, had been set as God's King upon the holy hill of the celestial Zion; He had asked of the Father, and had received the heathen nations of the world for

---

[1] Ps. ii. 2 ff.; cf. Acts iv. 23 ff.

His own. A rough and intractable flock, needing often to feel the sharpness of the iron with which the shepherd's staff was tipped! A misshapen vessel not meet for the Master's use, needing to be broken up into a thousand fragments that a new and better might take its place! As the first generation looked out upon the world of which the Christ-King had gone to take possession, these words of the second Psalm seemed exactly to describe the process by which His authority would be established. He was born to rule all the nations with the iron rod,[1] and even to smite them with the sharp sword of His mouth;[2] it was to be the reward of victory for members of the Church to bear their part in the grim work that lay before Him: *he that overcometh and keepeth my works unto the end, to him will I give authority over the nations; and he shall rule them with a rod of iron, as the vessels of the potter are broken to shivers, as I also have received of my Father.*[3] There is nothing in the Apocalypse more magnificent than its repeated acceptance of the difficult conditions under which the world was to be won by Christ, and by those faithful members of His Church to whom He should delegate His authority. Wherever the Seer looked, he saw either the hostile Empire, or beyond its borders fierce untamed tribes who inspired the provincials with alarm. But the reign

[1] Apoc. xii. 5. [2] Apoc. xix. 15. [3] Apoc. ii. 26 f.

THE KING

of Christ must go forwards,[1] and the Church continue her work on earth until all nations, within the Empire or beyond it, were subjugated to the obedience of faith. It may be an outburst of human impatience that demands to see within a single generation the world strewn with the wreckage of a shattered heathenism, but it is a Divine inspiration that will not let men rest till this has been accomplished. Meanwhile there is in the best Christian lives a power which, within narrow limits and on a small scale, exerts Christ's authority —the power of His Spirit which, in itself indomitable, bears down all opposition and in the end triumphs over it. This is never more remarkable than when it is seen in obscure unambitious lives, which, while following in the steps of Christ's sufferings, are at the same time marked by a dignity, a strength, and a victorious purpose that tell of their union with His life in heaven.

To S. John at the end of the first century a thousand years seemed an epoch long enough to allow for the reign of the Saints with Christ on earth. Now that the history of the Church is running to the end of its second millennium, there are those who tell us that the human race is but just entering upon its life, and has before it countless

[1] One after another of the early *Acta martyrum*, after dating the martyr's death by the years of the reigning Emperor, ends with the inspiring words *regnante Jesu Christo*.

ages of developement. Believers in the Ascen.
can entertain this possibility without uneasine
They can witness the material progress of ⟨
world without the suspicion that it may supersede
the spiritual sovereignty of Christ. They know that
He must reign till His rod of iron has done its work
on earth, and all enemies are put under His feet.

The reign of the Ascended Christ has a time limit.
This point has been worked out by S. Paul in a
passage which is not without difficulty. *Then (i.e.
at the Parousia) cometh the end, when he shall deliver
up the kingdom to God, even the Father ... for he must
reign till he* (the Father) *hath put all his enemies
under his feet. ... And when all things have been
subjected unto him, then shall the Son also himself be
subjected to him that did subject all things unto him, that
God may be all in all.*[1] With the foreseen end there
comes into view in this place the purpose of our
Lord's present reign. It is seen to be a temporary
economy, a parenthesis in God's great scheme of
things, called for by the lapse of a part of the
creation from its obedience to the Divine King. It
is a regency rather than a reign, a vice-royalty,
taking for the time the place of direct government.[2]

---

[1] 1 Cor. xv. 24 ff.

[2] This temporary kingdom is, of course, to be distinguished from the kingdom which belongs to the Son as one with the Father, of which the Creed, following Lc. i. 33, says: 'Of whose kingdom there shall no end.' See Pearson (ed. Burton, i. p. 335; ii. p. 240 f.).

had not Sin entered the cosmos, and Death, in its spiritual significance, followed Sin, no such episode in the eternal *Regnum Dei* would have been necessary. The circumstances demanded, it appears, a delegation of the Father's authority over all creation to the Incarnate Son, for the purpose of reducing His rebel creatures to their obedience. The Son, having entered the creation by taking our flesh, and having in that flesh overcome Sin and Death, completes His mission by receiving the submission of all creatures to Himself as the Father's Representative and Plenipotentiary. But the submission completed, or the enemies that refuse submission destroyed, He will no longer retain the authority which He received as the Christ; and as the Incarnate Son, He will lead Creation in the final subjection to the Father, which fulfils the purpose of the Christian economy. Then the great end will have been reached, and *God* will again be *all in all—God*, not the Father alone, but in the fulness of the Divine Name—Father, Son, and Holy Spirit; His Name hallowed, His Kingdom come, His will done, as in heaven so on earth.

This is the goal to which all history and life are moving, and for which the Ascension and the Session were the starting-point. The reign of the Ascended Christ is preparatory to the Eternal Reign of God.

III.

THE PRIEST.

THE Christ-King is also the Christ-Priest. That the two offices should meet in one person belongs to the Hebrew ideal both of priesthood and of kingship. This comes to light first in the old story of Melchizedek, King of Salem and *priest of God most High*.[1] 'The intention of the passage seems to be to represent him as the forerunner and prototype of the Israelite monarchy and Israelite priesthood.'[2] One prototype served for both, as if to shew that monarchy and priesthood are essentially one. There was a period in the history of the Jewish people when this ideal was nearly realized. From B.C. 142 till the rise of the Herod dynasty Judaea was ruled by a succession of High Priests, who were also civil governors—the priest-princes of the Hasmonaean line. In Christian times the mediaeval Papacy claimed to gather into its own hands the reins of all authority, temporal and ecclesiastical; for although

[1] Gen. xiv. 18 ff.   [2] Driver, *Genesis, ad loc.*

THE PRIEST

the exercise of the temporal power was usually committed to the Emperor, the Pope, it was said, held both swords.[1] Both experiments, the Jewish and the Christian, failed; and so far as can be judged from these examples, neither the temporal nor the spiritual interests of men are promoted by entrusting them to the care of the same representative. The double task is too great for mere man to discharge.

Yet it was precisely this union of sovereignty and priesthood, of the *imperium* and the *sacerdotium*, that the writer of the 110th Psalm in the Spirit foresaw to be the distinguishing mark of the Messianic Kingdom. He attributes this policy to Jahveh Himself:

> *Jahveh saith unto my Lord,*
> '*Sit thou at my right hand,*
> *Until I make thine enemies thy footstool.*'
>
> . . . . .
>
> *Jahveh hath sworn and will not repent,*
> '*Thou art a priest for ever,*
> *After the order of Melchizedek.*'[2]

In other words, in the good time which is coming there is to be a reversion to the original type of priest-kingship. The union of the two offices in one man was good, if only the man could be found who

---

[1] See this point well worked out in Canon Hobhouse's Bampton Lectures, *The Church and the World*, p. 190 ff.

[2] Psalm cx. 1, 4.

could bear the double burden. Such a man would be found, the Psalmist believed, in the ideal King of Israel. He has been found, the Church knows, in the Ascended Christ.

As the Apocalypse is largely a vision of Christ the King, so the Epistle to the Hebrews is our chief guide in all things relating to Christ the Priest. It is remarkable that S. Paul, notwithstanding his frequent insistence on the mediatorial work of our Lord, does not once call him 'High Priest' or 'Priest,' nor does he in any passage examine at length the relation of the Ascension to our Lord's priestly functions. It is possible that he was kept from developing his soteriology in this direction by the danger of misapprehension on the part of his Gentile readers, to whom sacrificial and hierarchical terms might have conveyed impressions reflected from their heathen surroundings. The author of Hebrews had no such fear; the Old Testament account of the Tabernacle and its ritual supplied illustrations of his argument, and there were no memories of pagan sacrifices or priesthood that could be awakened in the minds of Hebrew Christian readers. In any case, it was to this unknown teacher, and not to S. Paul, that it was given to deliver to the Church the great Christian doctrine of the High Priesthood of the Ascended Christ. We will endeavour to follow his guidance.

1. At the outset of the Epistle the Priest-King is

seen preparing for His priestly work in heaven. Before the Ascension He offered His one great Sacrifice, and thus *made purification of sins*.[1] But the preparation began further back, with the Incarnation. The Eternal Son partook of our flesh and blood, laying hold not on the nature of angels, but on the seed of Abraham.[2] He could not represent man to God, or offer sacrifice for man, unless He Himself were made man; nor could He succour tempted humanity unless He knew by experience what temptation meant.

The author next proceeds to connect the Incarnation and the Sacrifice with the Ascension.[3] Our High Priest *passed through the heavens* (διεληλυθότα τοὺς οὐρανούς), through court after court of the spiritual precincts, the Tabernacle not made with hands, until He reached the presence-chamber of God. There, in the inmost sanctuary, He now ministers. But His sinlessness and present remoteness from human infirmity imply no want of sympathy with our moral weaknesses (μὴ δυνάμενον συνπαθῆσαι ταῖς ἀσθενείαις ἡμῶν); although He is now on the Throne, it is a *throne of grace* to which the tempted and sinful may come with confidence.

2. The way is now cleared for a nearer view of our High Priest's functions and life in heaven.[4]

[1] Heb. i. 3. [2] Heb. ii. 14 ff.
[3] Heb. iv. 14 f. [4] Heb. v. 1, viii. 3.

Speaking generally, (*a*) a high priest in earthly communities is a person appointed to deal representatively with man's relations to God (τὰ πρὸς τὸν θεόν), and his chief business is to offer sacrifices both eucharistic and propitiatory (δῶρά τε καὶ θυσίας περὶ ἁμαρτιῶν). (*b*) In the case of all merely human priests, the holder of the office has need to offer for his own sins as well as for those of his people. (*c*) Although in later Jewish history high priests were made and deposed by popular vote or at the will of the civil ruler, the office originally and properly rests upon Divine appointment, and cannot be rightly assumed without a Divine call.

Now (to take the last point first), the Messiah had received such a call, being *named of God* (in the Psalter) *a high priest after the order of Melchizedek*.[1] But, as the analogy of Melchizedek suggests, He differs in many respects from other high priests. He is, like Melchizedek, a unique Person, not a member of a sacerdotal caste, but the solitary representative of His order. Like Melchizedek, again, He has no successor, because He is endowed with an endless life, and His priesthood is perpetual (εἰς τὸν αἰῶνα).[2] So it appears why the Psalm does not call Him a priest 'after the order of Aaron.' The Aaronic order was a succession of dying men who administered a transitory system, whereas the Risen and Ascended

[1] Heb. v. 10.   [2] Heb. vii. 8-19.

THE PRIEST

Christ is alive for evermore, and all His acts have the note of an indissoluble vitality (κατὰ δύναμιν ζωῆς ἀδιαλύτου). Thus this one utterance of the 110th Psalm sweeps away the whole structure of the Levitical ministry, substituting for it the undying life and work of the Royal Priest of the Gospel. It involves, on the one hand, the abolition of a Law which could bring nothing to perfection, and, on the other hand, the introduction into human life of something infinitely better, the great Hope through which we draw nigh to God in Christ (ἀθέτησις μὲν γίνεται ... ἐντολῆς ... ἐπεισαγωγὴ δὲ ἐλπίδος).

Further, our High Priest is not like the Levitical high priests, a sinner, but *holy, guileless, undefiled.*[1] He is not on earth, but *made higher than the heavens, a minister of the Sanctuary and of the True Tabernacle.* There He serves not *that which is a copy and shadow of the heavenly things,* but *the heavenly things themselves,* which needed to be cleansed *with better sacrifices*[2] than the blood of bulls and goats. His Sacrifice is one, and once offered. But if the sacrificial offering is not to be repeated, the Sacrifice remains, for it is identical with the Priest, and the Priest lives and ministers age after age in the heavenly Sanctuary of which the earthly was the antitype.[3]

3. Hence, although our Lord's priesthood is of the

---

[1] Heb. vii. 26. [2] Heb. viii. 5 (ix. 23).
[3] Heb. ix. 24 ἀντίτυπα τῶν ἀληθινῶν.

Melchizedekian and not the Aaronic type, yet we may look to the ritual of the Levitical sanctuary to throw light upon His priestly work in heaven. Even the structure of the Tabernacle has something to teach us. 'Cosmic' though it was,[1] it betokened that which is above and beyond the cosmos. It consisted of two tents in one, an outer and an inner. Before the entrance of each there hung a curtain; when you passed the first curtain, you were in the Holies ($\tau\grave{a}$ $\mathring{a}\gamma\iota a$); when you passed the second, you entered the Holiest ($\mathring{a}\gamma\iota a$ $\mathring{a}\gamma\iota\omega\nu$). The first had a lamp-stand, the second was left in darkness, and it was entered by no one but by the High Priest, and by him but once a year. In neither of these compartments was there ever any victim sacrificed; the place of sacrifice was in an outer enclosure which shut off the Tent of Meeting from the wilderness that lay around it.[2]

Such a sanctuary must have been to some extent symbolical, for it was clearly more elaborate than the exigencies of the wilderness-life demanded. Its name gives the clue to the meaning of the design. The *Tent of Meeting*,[3] as it is often called in Exodus and Numbers, is usually interpreted as the place

---

[1] Heb. ix. 1 τό τε ἅγιον κοσμικόν.

[2] See Westcott 'on the general significance of the Tabernacle.' (Add. Note on Heb. viii. 5.)

[3] See Exod. xxv. 22, xxix. 42, xxx. 36. For other explanations of אֹהֶל מוֹעֵד see Driver on Deut. xxxi. 14 f., and M'Neil on Exod. xxxiii. 7.

THE PRIEST

where God met Moses and His people, and the structure, it would seem, represented the process by which God draws near to man and man to God. The Court, the Holies, the Holiest, symbolized successive stages in the approach; the curtains which veiled the Court from the outer world, the Holies from the Court and the Holiest from the Holies, and the darkness and inaccessibility of the Holiest, all proclaimed that the way into the presence of God was not yet made manifest to the world or, in its completeness, even to Israel or to the priests of the Law. On the other hand, the yearly entrance of the High Priest pointed to some great revelation in the future, some breaking of bounds and rending of veils, after which access to the Holiest would become general, and all Israel be free to enter at all times where their representative hitherto had entered but once in the twelve months.

Three great writers of the first century set themselves to the task of reading the symbolism of the Tabernacle. To Josephus[1] it was a representation of the mystery of earth, sea, and sky. Philo of Alexandria[2] saw further; in his view the outer court is the phenomenal world ($\tau\grave{a}$ $a\grave{i}\sigma\theta\eta\tau\acute{a}$), and the sanctuary, the intellectual ($\tau\grave{a}$ $\nu o\eta\tau\acute{a}$); in the person of the high priest, the cosmos is seen feeling its

---
[1] Josephus, *Antt.* iii. 7. 7; *Bell. Jud.* v. 5. 4 ff.
[2] Philo, *vita Moysis*, iii. 14. I owe the references to Westcott, *op. cit.*

way into that which lies beyond both sensation and the province of the intellect. Lastly, the Christian writer of Hebrews finds the key to the puzzle in the Christian faith. But in his use of the key he limits himself almost entirely to a single point, the ritual of the Day of Atonement, and to such details of the ritual as are directly illustrative of the Lord's priestly work in heaven.

4. The sacrifices of that day, as of every other day throughout the year, were offered in the outer court: the blood of the sacrificed animals alone was carried by the high priest within the Holiest. So our Lord's great Sacrifice was offered by Him on earth, not, however, in heathen lands, but within the enclosure of the land of Israel. But having offered it, He passed in right of the atoning blood into heaven itself, there *to appear before the face of God for us.* The entrance was made, as the Sacrifice was offered, once for all; the whole period of time from the Ascension to the Return is one age-long Day of Atonement. The true Atonement for sin exceeds the figure in every particular; it is permanent and does not need yearly renewal; it avails for the sins of the whole world and not only of a single people; it effects a moral and not only a ceremonial taking away of sin, purifying the conscience from the deadness that paralyses spiritual activity.[1] But if

[1] Heb. ix. 24.

THE PRIEST

the Blood of Christ is potent in the lives of men on earth, it is yet more potent in heaven, in the hands of the Great High Priest. Heaven is not a place of sacrifice, and our Lord is no longer, strictly speaking, a Sacrificing Priest; He has *offered one sacrifice for sins for ever*.[1] But His presence in the Holiest is a perpetual and effective presentation before God of the Sacrifice once offered, which is no less needful for our acceptance than the actual death upon the Cross. He has indeed *somewhat to offer* in His heavenly priesthood,[2] for He offers Himself as representing to God man reconciled, and as claiming for man the right of access to the Divine presence.[3] He Himself, as He sits on the Throne, in the perfected and glorified Manhood which has been obedient unto death, is the living Propitiation for our sins, and the standing guarantee of acceptance to all *that draw near unto God through him*.[4]

5. In one other respect the analogy of the Jewish high priest falls far short of the Christian counterpart. The high priest of Israel entered the Holiest alone, the congregation remaining in the outer court till he came back to them: if they had access

---

[1] Heb. x. 12.

[2] See Dr. W. Milligan, *Ascension of our Lord*, p. 120 f.

[3] See Westcott on 'the present work of Christ as High Priest' (Add. Note on Heb. viii. 1 f.); Prof. G. Milligan, *Theology of Hebrews*, p. 141 ff.

[4] Heb. vii. 25.

to God meanwhile, this was only through their representative. But the author of Hebrews will not allow that the Church, while awaiting the Return of her High Priest, is compelled to remain without. Not only have believers entered the Holiest in the person of their Representative, but they themselves may enter in His Name. The thick curtain still hangs before the Sanctuary: the Holiest is still dark and inscrutable; the Christian faith has not yet illuminated the ultimate mysteries of life. But since the Ascension there is a way through the veil: a Way new and living ($\pi\rho\acute{o}\sigma\phi\alpha\tau o\varsigma$ $\kappa\alpha\grave{\iota}$ $\zeta\hat{\omega}\sigma\alpha$), the Incarnate, Sacrificed, Risen, Ascended Christ. Thus the author can end his long exposition with the practical counsel: *Having therefore, brethren, boldness to enter into the holy place by the blood of Jesus, by the way which he dedicated for us ... and having a great Priest over the House of God, let us draw near with a true heart in fulness of faith.*[1] This is the issue of the whole doctrine of our Lord's highpriestly life in heaven. It has secured to every human being free and direct access to God. This access is not, indeed, immediate, as it is sometimes represented to be; it is mediated by Christ, and in ways of His appointment. But it is so real and falls so well within the range of Christian experience that every believer can test for himself

[1] Heb. x. 19 ff.

the truth of our Lord's work in heaven, however little he can discern its nature. Communion with God through Christ in the Holy Spirit is not a theory or a dogma, but a fact of personal knowledge to which tens of thousands of living Christians can testify as the most certain of actualities.

6. Yet this freedom of access to God is not all that our Lord's priesthood has gained for us. The New Testament—for here we need not limit ourselves to the Epistle to the Hebrews—claims that He has made us sharers in His priestly life. We come to God through Him, not merely as suppliants or worshippers, but as priests. The new Israel, like the Israel of the Exodus, is a consecrated race, a *holy priesthood, to offer up spiritual sacrifices acceptable to God through Jesus Christ.*[1] He not only *loosed us from our sins by his blood,* but *made us ... priests unto his God and Father. Thou ... didst purchase unto God with thy blood,* the Elders sing before the Throne, *men of every tongue and people and nation, and madest them to be unto our God ... priests.* The saints of the First Resurrection shall be *priests of God and of Christ,* ministering both to the Father and to the Incarnate and glorified Son.[2] They offer themselves, their souls and bodies, *a living sacrifice, holy, acceptable to God,* their *spiritual* (λογικήν) *service.*[3] They offer the *sacrifice of praise continually, that is, the*

[1] 1 Pet. ii. 5.   [2] Apoc. i. 5 f., v. 9, xx. 6.   [3] Rom. xii. 1.

fruit of lips which make confession to his name. They offer all good and unselfish actions,[1] for *with such sacrifices God is well pleased.*[2] Thus the whole Christian life is a succession of priestly acts, of sacrifices which the Church is privileged to offer to God through Christ. The Church is a priesthood, but not a sacerdotal caste; Jew and Gentile, bond and free, nations of all tongues and habits of life, are admitted to it on the sole condition of faith in Jesus Christ and baptism into Him. The special priesthood of the Christian clergy is the priesthood of the Body exercised through its officers, and expressing itself in official acts, especially in those of common worship and its culminating rite, the Holy Eucharist.

7. There can be no reasonable doubt that the Eucharist stands in a very special relation both to the Sacrifice of the Death of Christ and to His priestly Self-presentation in heaven. Our Lord's own words of instruction give this great Sacrament a double character. On one side it is an act of Communion: *take, eat ... drink ye all of it*, can leave no doubt upon this point. One of the greatest blessings which the Reformation of the sixteenth century brought to the Church of England was the restoration to the laity of the Cup which is the Blood of the Covenant; perhaps the most

---

[1] τῆς εὐποιίας καὶ κοινωνίας.   [2] Heb. xiii. 15 f.

hopeful factor in the religious movements of the nineteenth century has been the widespread return of religious Church-people to the primitive practice of weekly Communion. But the emphasis thus laid upon the act of Communion must not be suffered to divert attention from the other revealed purpose of the Sacrament. It is also an act of Commemoration; He who said *Take, eat ... drink*, said also, *This do for my memorial* (εἰς τὴν ἐμὴν ἀνάμνησιν).[1] This act of Commemoration, so far as we can see, is intended to be the Church's counterpart on earth to the Self-presentation of our Lord in heaven.[2] Neither in heaven nor on earth can there be any repetition of the Sacrifice, but only a presentation before God of the One full, perfect, and sufficient Offering. In heaven this presentation is made by the Ascended Christ Himself. *I saw in the midst of the Throne ... a Lamb standing as though it had been slain. Worthy art thou ... for thou wast slain ... worthy is the Lamb that hath been slain*:[3] so the Elders and the Angels recognize the abiding sacrificial value of the Ascended Life. On earth the Church, by Christ's

---

[1] So ἀνάμνησις is used in Lev. xxiv. 7, Num. x. 10. But the usual word for a memorial before God in the LXX is μνημόσυνον, so that it is precarious to press ἀνάμνησις in this sense. Nor is it so used liturgically: see Gore, *Body of Christ*, p. 315 f.

[2] W. Milligan, *Ascension*, p. 266: [communicants] "transact here below what He is transacting in the heavenly Sanctuary."

[3] Apoc. v. 6, 9, 12.

ordinance, commemorates the Sacrifice under the form of Bread and Wine, and thus *proclaims the Lord's death till he come*. The presentation in heaven, the commemoration on earth, will go on simultaneously up to the moment of the Lord's Return. The Eucharistic commemoration is not, indeed, described in Scripture as a presentation of our Lord's sacrifice to God : S. Paul's *proclaim* (καταγγέλλετε) refers rather to the witness borne by it to the world and the Church. But our solemn memorial is assuredly made in the presence of God, and before all the company of heaven ; and it proclaims the Death of the Lord, not as a past event, as we might commemorate the death of a martyr, but as a Sacrifice which lives on and is perpetually presented by Christ Himself in heaven. *We have an altar*[1] which answers to the heavenly Altar at which the Great High Priest officiates. The Eucharistic rite is the nearest approach which the priestly Body of Christ on earth can make to a participation in the High-priestly Self-presentation of her Head in heaven. Hence it is that all spiritual sacrifices meet in this supreme Christian service—the offering of alms and

---

[1] The words of Heb. xiii. 10, though admitting of a wider interpretation, cannot but have an Eucharistic reference. "The 'Table' of the Lord (1 Cor. x. 21), the Bread and Wine, enabled the believers to 'show forth Christ's Death'... in this Sacrament, thus, ... the Christian has that which more than fulfils the types of the Jewish ritual" (Westcott, *ad loc.*).

THE PRIEST

oblations, the offering of praise and thanksgiving, the offering of souls and bodies. No Liturgy has more fully emphasized this concurrence of sacrificial acts in the Eucharist than the Anglican Order of Holy Communion, though the circumstances of the sixteenth century imposed upon our Reformers some necessary reserve as to the use of sacrificial language which the ancient Church could freely employ.

No aspect of our Lord's heavenly life is more to be insisted upon than His priestly office and work. Popular theology on all sides shews a tendency to stop short at the Cross, that is, at the historical moment when the Divine Sacrifice was offered.[1] The blessings of our redemption are traced to the Passion with such exclusive insistence as to suggest that they would have been ours if Christ had neither risen from the dead nor ascended into heaven. The whole attitude of the Christian life is affected by this departure from the primitive teaching; a dead Christ instead of a living Lord becomes the object of devotion: the anchor of the soul is fixed in the past and not in the present and future. The error, as in many other instances, turns upon the disproportionate weight which is attached to certain familiar words of Holy Scripture, while others, which are necessary to preserve the balance of truth, are strangely over-

---
[1] Cf. the remarks of W. Milligan, *op. cit.*, p. 129.

looked. Thus the words, *It is finished*,[1] are supposed to exclude atoning work of any kind subsequent to the death of the Cross; whereas they only announce the completion of the particular work of obedience unto death which was the purpose of our Lord's earthly life. Neither the analogy of the Old Testament Day of Atonement, nor the direct teaching of the New Testament, sanctions the doctrine that the priestly work of Christ was finished when He died. If He was *delivered for our trespasses*, He was *raised for our justification*; if we were *reconciled to God through the death of his Son, much more... shall we be saved by his life*.[2] With S. Paul not the Cross and Passion, but the Ascension and the High-priestly Intercession are the climax of our Lord's saving work.

If we ask what are the forces making for the salvation of men that flow from the priestly life of Christ in heaven, the answer may well be, What saving powers are there which do not proceed from it? All that the sacrifice of His earthly life obtained for us men and for our salvation, His heavenly High-priestly life bestows upon us. The whole life of grace in the Church on earth springs from this source; the Sacraments derive their whole efficacy from it; all the *greater works* that the Church has done since the Ascension—the baptism of the nations into Christ,

---

[1] Jo. xix. 30 (τετέλεσται, *consummatum est*).
[2] Rom. iv. 25, v. 10, viii.

the interpenetration of human life and thought with the mind of Christ, the splendid victories of Christian faith and love, have been possible only because our High Priest has gone on our behalf into the Holiest, and there perpetually presents Himself to God. A gospel which ended with the story of the Cross would have had all the elevating power of infinite pathos and love. But the power of an endless life would have been wanting. It is the abiding life of our High Priest which makes His atoning Sacrifice operative, and is the unfailing spring of the life of justification and grace in all His true members upon earth.

IV.

THE PROPHET.

THE Christ-offices are commonly reckoned as three; with the royal and the high-priestly life the Lord's Anointed unites the character of Prophet. There are examples in the Old Testament of the Prophet-King, the Prophet-Priest, and the Priest-King. But the fulness of Christhood seems to have been reserved for the ideal King and Priest and Prophet, who is able in His human life to discharge the functions of all.[1]

At first sight it might appear that the Lord's office of Prophet ceased when He left this earth. While His kingdom is not of this world, and His High-priestly work finds its proper sphere in the Holiest, the prophetic office might seem to have no place in a world where the full light of God streams upon all the inhabitants, and no interpretation of the Divine will can be needed. In the days of His flesh, on the

[1] There are, however, approaches to this exercise of the three functions in the life of David, who was a prophet (2 Sam. xxiii. 2; cf. Acts ii. 30), and on one occasion assumed the ephod (2 Sam. vi. 14).

THE PROPHET

other hand, the Christ was pre-eminently Prophet; even those who were outside the circle of His disciples knew Him for this,[1] and our Lord accepted the title,[2] for, so far as it went, it was a true description of His work. His whole teaching was prophetic—*a new teaching*,[3] if not in all its contents, yet in its searching inwardness, in its creative power, in the Divine authority which He manifestly claimed. It must have been among the overwhelming sorrows which lay upon the souls of the Eleven on the night before the Passion, that the voice which had spoken as never man spake was about to be silenced in death. Jesus left nothing in writing, and all that remained of the utterances of the greatest prophet that Israel or the world had known was but an uncertain memory preserved by a group of loyal but imperfectly taught followers.

So indeed it seemed to the Apostles. But even on that last night their Prophet taught them to look forward to a renewal of His teaching. His previous instructions had been but the first instalment of a greater prophecy, fuller, plainer, and more satisfactory than any hitherto uttered. *These things have I spoken unto you in proverbs* (ἐν παροιμίαις); *the hour cometh when I shall no more speak unto you in proverbs, but shall tell you plainly* (παρρησίᾳ ἀπαγγελῶ) *of the*

[1] Cf. Mc. vi. 15, Jo. iv. 19, vi. 14, ix. 17.   [2] Mc. vi. 4.
[3] Mc. i. 27.

Father.[1] The teaching of the Ministry had been on the whole parabolic or paroemiac—a revelation half revealed, draped in the wrappings of figure and symbol that hid the brightness of the naked truth, on which even the Eleven could not as yet bear to look.[2] When Christ was taken from them, the plainer teaching of their Prophet would begin; not indeed as they understood 'plainness,'[3] that is, with an apparent simplicity which veiled unapprehended realities, but by way of a direct appeal to spiritually enlightened understandings, giving them an insight into the inmost truth of things. Thus, the Christ-Prophet's larger and directer teachings were to belong to His life with the Father and not to His brief Ministry among men.

The same discourse revealed to the Apostles the means by which the Lord would continue to teach after His departure. *These things have I spoken unto you while abiding with you; but the Paraclete, even the Holy Spirit, whom the Father will send in my name, he shall teach you all things, and bring to your remembrance all things that I said unto you. When he, the Spirit of truth, is come, he shall guide you into all the truth: for he shall not speak from*

---

[1] Jo. xvi. 25.   [2] Jo. xvi. 12 οὐ δύνασθε βαστάζειν ἄρτι.

[3] Cf. verse 29, νῦν ἐν παρρησίᾳ λαλεῖς, though He had just used words (ἐξῆλθον—ἐλήλυθε—ἀφίημι—πορεύομαι) which were really as hard to understand as any of His earlier sayings.

himself (ἀφ' ἑαυτοῦ); *but what things soever he shall hear, these shall he speak: and he shall declare unto you the things that are to come.*[1] If it be said that according to these statements it is the Spirit who is the Prophet of the present dispensation and not the Son, the answer is that the Spirit of Christ and Christ Himself are one in operation; for though the Spirit is *another Paraclete*, and not identical with the Son, yet in the mysterious life of God the acts and words of each Person of the Holy Trinity are those of the Three, and the Spirit of the Son, as the Teacher of truth, is not to be distinguished from the Son whose Spirit He is. Jesus Christ, then, is still the Prophet of the Church, teaching her now by His Spirit as He taught during His earthly life by His own human voice.

As far back as the earliest days of the Ministry, it was recognized by John the Baptist that a greater Baptist had arisen in the person of the Christ; *he shall baptize you with the Holy Spirit.*[2] The Synoptic Gospels place this testimony at the beginning of their record, but make no further reference to it, for the fulfilment of John's prediction did not fall within their scope. The fourth Gospel, with other aims, recurs frequently to the baptism of the Spirit, ending with the anticipatory gift of the Spirit to the Church

---
[1] Jo. xiv. 25 f., xvi. 13 f.
[2] Mc. i. 8 (Mt. iii. 11, Lc. iii. 16).

on the night after the Resurrection.¹ The writer is conscious, however, that the gift could not be received in its fulness till the Son had returned to the Father: *as yet* (he says) *there was no Spirit, because Jesus was not as yet glorified* (οὔπω ἦν πνεῦμα ὅτι Ἰησοῦς οὔπω ἐδοξάσθη).²

The glorification of the Son of Man was succeeded almost immediately by the Coming of the Spirit. The world received visible and audible evidence of the Ascension in the works and utterances of the promised Paraclete: the Christ, S. Peter claims, *being ... by the right hand of God exalted, and having received of the Father the promise of the Holy Spirit, he hath poured forth this, which ye now see and hear.*³ The Baptism of the Spirit had begun, to continue so long as the Incarnate Son is with the Father. For the presence of the Spirit with the Church is the complement of the presence of the Son in heaven, a "vicarious power"⁴ which fills the place of the absent Lord and makes Him spiritually present with us, and by which He speaks and teaches to the end of time. *I come unto you.... I have yet many things to say unto you.... I will see you again.*⁵ So the Lord

---

¹cc. i., iii., iv., vi., vii., xiv.—xvi., xx.

²Jo. vii. 39.   ³Acts ii. 33.

⁴Tertullian, *de praescr.* 13 vicariam vim Spiritus sancti. *De virg. vel.* i. vicario domini Spiritu sancto.

⁵Jo. xiv. 18, xvi. 12, 22.

THE PROPHET

speaks in His last discourse, and the Spirit fulfils His words. The prophetic office of the Ascended Christ is realized in the experience of the Spirit-taught Church.

1. In the first age this office manifested itself in a new gift of prophecy. The Christian Prophets of the first age were second only to the Apostles as foundation stones in the building of the Church.[1] It would probably be an error to suppose that the somewhat erratic and effusive manifestations which S. Paul endeavoured to bring under control at Corinth were the normal fruits of the prophetic Spirit. The first efforts of Christianity to grapple with the problems of Greek life were made under conditions which tended to keep the standard of spiritual attainment low in cities such as Corinth and Thessalonica.[2] Our estimate of the place which prophecy held in the Apostolic Church must be formed on a wider view of its work. We must not forget the prophets and teachers in the Church at Antioch who, as they *ministered to the Lord and fasted*, received the inspiration which prompted the first great mission to the Gentile world, nor the probability that Barnabas and Saul themselves were of their number. Judas and Silas, who were chosen to interpret to the Church at

---

[1] 1 Cor. xii. 28, Eph. iv. 11 (cf. ii. 20 ἐποικοδομηθέντας ἐπὶ τῷ θεμελίῳ τῶν ἀποστόλων καὶ προφητῶν.

[2] Cf. 1 Cor. xiv. 26 ff. and 1 Thess. v. 20 προφητείας μὴ ἐξουθενεῖτε.

Antioch the great decision of the mother-church, on which the future of Gentile Christendom depended, were *themselves also prophets*.¹ To an Ephesian prophet we owe the priceless Apocalypse of S. John, and it is clear from his book how great was the influence of the prophets of his time in the churches of the great province of Asia. In S. John's eyes the *Spirit of prophecy* and the *testimony of Jesus* were identical.² Even in reference to the Corinthian prophets S. Paul had found himself able to write: *He that prophesieth speaketh unto men edification and comfort and consolation.... If all prophesy, and there come in one unbelieving or unlearned, he is reproved by all, he is judged by all, the secrets of his heart are made manifest; and so he will fall down on his face and worship God, declaring that God is among you indeed*.³

Such was early Christian prophecy at its best. Is the gift extinct? In one sense *prophecies*, as it seems, are *done away*;⁴ the manifestations described in the letters to Corinth subsided, and after some fitful recoveries, disappeared. But the Church retains what is essential: not only have we the New Testament records of first century inspiration, but

---

[1] Acts xiii. 1 ff., xv. 27, 32.
[2] Apoc. xix. 10 ἡ γὰρ μαρτυρία Ἰησοῦ ἐστὶν τὸ πνεῦμα τῆς προφητείας.
[3] 1 Cor. xiv. 3, 24.
[4] 1 Cor. xiii. 8 αἱ προφητεῖαι καταργηθήσονται.

THE PROPHET

the power of the prophetic Spirit makes itself felt in the great books, the stirring words, the quickening and uplifting influence of the best Christian teachers, whether priests or laymen. There have been within our own memory writers, preachers, workers, before whom the secrets of men's hearts have been made manifest, whose words and lives have compelled many to declare that God is among His people indeed. The prophetic order may have ceased or have been suspended, but the Spirit of prophecy still bears witness to the prophetic office of the Ascended Christ in the teaching of the living Church.

2. But the work of Christ the Prophet extends far beyond the small circle of teachers who possess a gift of inspiration. It is carried on continuously through the whole Church, regarded as the Witness and Keeper of the word of God, the *pillar and ground of the truth*.[1] *When he, the Spirit of truth, is come* (so our Lord has promised), *he shall guide you into all the truth*.[2] It cannot be believed that this promise was limited to one age or to one succession of Bishops. Neither the Apostolic age nor the Roman See was by Christ's gift invested with a monopoly of infallible guidance. The gift belongs to the whole Body of Christ, and it is converted into actuality by the gradual, age-long leading of the Spirit of Christ which dwells in the Body. It is a

---

[1] 1 Tim. iii. 15. [2] Jo. xvi. 13.

leading by which each age of the Church is brought, according to its measure, towards the fulness of the truth. Doubtless the Apostolic age was remarkable for the clearness of vision with which it was enabled to deliver to the Church once for all the essentials of Christian faith and life. But other ages have worked out with great success some particular doctrines of the faith, as the fourth and fifth centuries developed for all time the Christology of Catholic Christendom, and the sixteenth century endeavoured to resuscitate S. Paul's great doctrine of Justification by faith. Nor need we doubt that our own age is being led through many hitherto untried ways to the recovery of lost truths or to the formulation of truths which have hitherto been recognized or expressed only in part. We may be assured that no age, no teacher, has ever grasped *all the truth* with such completeness that nothing is left for the Spirit of Christ to teach, or for the Church to learn. The work of our Prophet is not ended, and will not be before His return. *I have yet,* He tells us, *many things to say unto you.* Meanwhile what are the great contents of the teaching of the Spirit of Christ?

The Lord Himself answers: I *shall tell you plainly of the Father.*[1] *Lord, shew us the Father* (said Philip, speaking for the Eleven), *and it sufficeth us* ;[2] the knowledge of the Father, the Source of all life and

---

[1] Jo. xvi. 25.   [2] Jo. xiv. 8.

THE PROPHET

love and of the Godhead itself, is the ultimate truth and the supreme satisfaction of the mind and heart of man. The Lord's answer to Philip is of extraordinary interest. *Have I been so long time with you, and dost thou not know me, Philip? He that hath seen me hath seen the Father; how sayest thou, Shew us the Father?*[1] How indeed, if during the years of the ministry he had come to know Jesus as He is? But this was what Philip and the rest had failed to do, and now the Spirit was coming to give that deeper knowledge which no length of acquaintance with Christ after the flesh could give. *He shall glorify me*, the Lord says later on in the same discourse, *for he shall take of mine, and shall declare* (ἀπαγγελεῖ) *it unto you*; adding, *All things whatsoever the Father hath are mine; therefore said I, that he taketh of mine, and shall declare it unto you.*[2] The Spirit of Christ thus reveals the Father by revealing the Son, for to know the Son is to know the Father also. This process of the revelation of the Father through the Son can be seen in nearly all the Epistles of the New Testament, but especially in the Epistles of S. Paul. S. Paul's Christ is none other than the Christ of the Synoptic Gospels and the Creeds: the human Christ who was *born of the seed of David*, and *born of a woman*, who suffered and died and was buried, and rose from the dead the third

[1] Jo. xiv. 9.   [2] Jo. xvi. 14 f.

day.¹ But while the gospel of the Nativity, the Cross, and the Resurrection was delivered by S. Paul *first of all* (ἐν πρώτοις) wherever he carried the faith, it was but the foundation on which he built, and not the whole or the chief part of the structure. As he builded, new views of the Lord's person and offices presented themselves to his mind, and were worked into the edifice. He came to know a Christ after the Spirit who existed before the worlds, who is *the Image of the invisible God*, in whom all things were created and all things consist;² a Christ who, *being in the form of God*, emptied Himself, taking the form of a servant, *becoming obedient unto death*, and thus earning for Himself in His human nature the Name which is above every name and the homage of the whole creation.³ Here indeed we see the Spirit glorifying Jesus by taking of that which is His and shewing it to the mind of the Apostle, and through him to the Church of all time. But this glorification of Jesus, it is evident, in no way disturbs the balance of the Apostle's monotheistic belief, on which the Gospel itself is based; *to us*, S. Paul protests, *there is but One God, the Father*. On the contrary, nowhere in the Bible is so large a place assigned to the Person of the Father as in the Pauline Epistles. *The God and Father of our Lord Jesus Christ, the Father of mercies and God of all comfort,*

---

[1] Rom. i. 3, Gal. iv. 4, 1 Cor. xv. 3 f. [2] Col. i. 15 f. [3] Phil. ii. 6 ff.

THE PROPHET

the Father who made us meet to be partakers of the inheritance of the saints in light, who hath blessed us with every spiritual blessing in the heavenly places in Christ, the Father of glory,[1] is everywhere presented as the Supreme Object of Christian faith and love and hope; and it is precisely in the Epistles of the Roman Captivity, which are distinguished by S. Paul's richest Christology, that the glory of the Father is most abundantly set forth. The Johannine writings exhibit the same remarkable connexion between the glorification of the Son and that of the Father; the fourth Gospel, with its far higher doctrine of the Person of Christ, has far more to say of the Father than the Synoptics, and the first Epistle of S. John is also singularly full of the theology of the First Person. Thus in revealing the Son the Spirit of Christ tells us plainly of the Father; in shewing us the things of Christ, He shews us the things of the Person who sent Him. So great is the mistake of those who minimize the Divine glory of the Son from a desire to emphasize the supremacy of the Father. Our conception of the glory of the Father does not lose but gains in proportion as we realize the glory of the Son; when men confess Jesus Christ to be Lord, they do so *to the glory of God the Father*; it is *in the face of Jesus Christ*, that *the light of the knowledge of the glory of God* is given.[2]

[1] 2 Cor. i. 3, Col. i. 12, Eph. I. 3, 17. [2] Phil. ii. 11, 2 Cor. iv. 6.

Christ our Prophet, then, shews us the Father by revealing Himself through the Spirit. He teaches His Church continually in the Apostolic writings, in the *consensus* of a truly Catholic tradition, in the creeds and confessions, the hymns and liturgies of Christendom, in the great theological works of Christian antiquity, in the effort which is made by each successive age to carry on the developement of religious thought; in the voice of the living Church, even, it may be, in voices which are not of the Church, but by which the Spirit of truth is guiding men into unsuspected approaches to the fuller knowledge of God.

3. The teaching of the Spirit of Christ is not, however, to be limited to Scripture and tradition, or to other channels of truth which are external to the personal life. If this were so, it could be accepted by a simple act of submission to authority, and its power over life would be proportionately small. A purely external revelation might conceivably serve many great purposes, but it could not of itself deeply stir the hearts of men. But the teaching of the Spirit of Christ is not external only; He enters the inner man, touches the springs of the moral nature, and makes it to respond to the external teaching of Scripture and the Church.

Ye have an anointing from the Holy One, so S. John writes to the members of the Apostolic Church,—

THE PROPHET

and ye know all things.[1] *I have not written unto you because ye know not the truth, but because ye know it.... The anointing which ye received of him abideth in you, and ye need not that any one teach you; but as his anointing teacheth you concerning all things ... and even as it taught you, ye abide in him.*[2] This is perhaps the *locus classicus* on the Inner Light, but it does not stand alone. Throughout the New Testament it is assumed that every believer is in his own measure *taught of God*.[3] Moses, when some feared that his office was being invaded by an outburst of prophecy in the camp, exclaimed, *Would God that all the Lord's people were prophets.*[4] In the new Israel the wish of the Lawgiver finds its fulfilment. As all the members of Christ are by their union with Him made kings and priests, so a measure of His Spirit of prophecy has descended on each of them. Not all Christians, indeed, are 'prophets' in the sense of possessing a special inspiration, but all have been *made to drink of one Spirit,* and all living members of Christ have learned what man cannot teach. Few things are more remarkable in the writings of S. Paul than the ungrudging recognition by so great an expert in Christian truth of the right inherent in all

---

[1] Or, according to another reading, *ye all know.*

[2] 1 John ii. 20, 27.

[3] See John vi. 45 f. (citing Isa. liv. 13), vii. 17, 1 Th. iv. 9.

[4] Num. xi. 29.

believers to know all that God has revealed through Christ, and his evident desire that they should rise to the fulness of their privilege. *I myself also am persuaded of you, my brethren*, he writes to the Roman Christians, whom he knew by report only, *that ye yourselves are ... filled with all knowledge, able also to admonish one another.*[1] *I bow my knees unto the Father*, he writes again to the churches of Asia, *that he would grant you ... that ye may be strengthened through his Spirit in the inward man; that Christ may dwell in your hearts through faith, to the end that ye ... may be strong to apprehend with all the saints ... and to know the love of Christ.*[2] Personal gifts differ widely, but a certain capacity for spiritual truth and apprehension of it belong to all who have the Spirit of Christ; a capacity which is sometimes the more remarkable because of the intellectual poverty of those who manifest it. Many a parish priest will thankfully admit that he has learnt from poor and simple folk among his flock lessons that no book can teach. Such unconscious teachers are witnesses to the power of the Spirit of Christ, who makes the humblest believers not only receptive of spiritual knowledge, but able in their measure to impart it.

In such ways as these the Ascended Christ still fulfils the office of Prophet, and fulfils it far more

[1] Rom. xv. 14.   [2] Eph. iii. 14 ff.

THE PROPHET

effectually and widely than was possible in the days of His flesh. Then *all things* were *done in parables, that seeing, men might see and not perceive*, and hearing, they might *hear and not understand.*[1] To the Church since the Pentecost *is given the mystery of the kingdom of God*; teaching by parables and proverbs has been exchanged for 'plainness of speech.' It is the same Christ who speaks, but He speaks now by the Spirit, and the voice of the Spirit reaches further and can teach more than the human voice of the greatest of masters. So the spiritual teaching of our race will be carried forward, till our Prophet returns, and takes up again in the ages to come that revelation of the Father in His own Person which He began when He *dwelt among us* in the days before the Cross.

[1] Mc. iv. 11 f.

V.

THE HEAD.

The Headship of the Ascended Lord is a Pauline conception which the Apostle works out at length only from one point of view. Hints are dropped that it admits of several applications. Christ is *Head of every man*, as the man is the head of the wife, and as God is the Head of Christ.[1] He is *the Head of every principality and authority* (πάσης ἀρχῆς καὶ ἐξουσίας); all the authorities of the unseen world as well as of the world of men are under His control.[2] He is *Head over all things to the Church*; He possesses an universal sovereignty which is exercised for the good of His Body.[3] It is evident that these suggestive statements open vast fields for speculative thought. But S. Paul has not entered upon them, and, it may be, has purposely abstained from the attempt. In one direction, however, he felt himself at liberty to go further, for it concerned the highest interests of

[1] 1 Cor. xi. 3.   [2] Col. ii. 10; cf. 1 Pet. iii. 22.
[3] Eph. i. 22; cf. Mt. xxviii. 18.

all Christians. The Ascended Christ is in a very special sense Head of the universal Church. Of this Headship the Apostle has much to say, and he says it in several passages which are among the most profoundly interesting in his great Epistles to the Ephesians and Colossians.[1]

Two lines of thought are open to us when we think of Christ as the Head of the Church. The title may represent either (1) the authority exercised by Him over the whole Christian Society, or (2) the relation in which He stands to the life of the Church, as a spiritual Body deriving its sustenance from Him.

1. The first of these aspects of our Lord's Headship is before the mind of S. Paul in a passage which deals with Christian marriage and married life.[2] *A husband*, he teaches, *is head of his wife, as also the Christ is Head of his Church*. It follows that, as the Church lives in subjection (ὑποτάσσεται) to the Christ, so the wives should be in every respect subject to their husbands. But it also follows that the husbands should use their authority for the good of their wives, and in the spirit of love. Christ is the Saviour of the Body of which He is Head. He loved the Church and delivered Himself to the death of the Cross for

---

[1] Eph. i. 22 f., iv. 15 f., v. 23 f.; Col. i. 18, ii. 19.
[2] Eph. v. 22 ff. ἀνήρ ἐστιν κεφαλὴ τῆς γυναικός (cf. 1 Cor. xi. 3), ὡς καὶ ὁ χριστὸς κεφαλὴ τῆς ἐκκλησίας.

her sake, His purpose being to consecrate and cleanse her by the sacramental bath of Baptism, and in the end to present her to Himself *glorious, not having spot* of defilement *or wrinkle* of age, or any such thing; that, in a word, she should be *holy and without blemish*[1] in the sight of God His Father, to whose presence He will bring her. Meanwhile her subordination is not servile, but the willing submission of the wife who obeys not only for conscience sake, but because she loves, reveres, and adores. Thus for Christians the marriage bond has become a *mystery*, and a great one,[2] for it reveals nothing less than 'the mystical union that is betwixt Christ and His Church'; authority on the part of Christ, subordination on the part of the Church, love on both sides—love answering to love, to be crowned by the fulness of joy when the union is consummated at the coming of the Lord.

Nothing in early Christianity is more admirable than this attitude of loving subjection to the Ascended Christ. *Jesus is Lord* was not only the creed of the Apostolic Church, but its rule of life. His members were ready to live or to die for Him—it scarcely seemed to matter which. *None of us*, S. Paul appeals

[1] Cf. Eph. i. 4.

[2] Eph. v. 32 τὸ μυστήριον τοῦτο μέγα ἐστίν (Vulg. *hoc sacramentum magnum est*). The 'heavenly archetype' of marriage, S. Paul would say, is 'the relation of Christ to the Ecclesia.' See Hort, *Ecclesia*, p. 152.

to his fellow-Christians, *liveth to himself*, and *none dieth to himself . . . whether we live, we live unto the Lord, or whether we die, we die unto the Lord: whether we live therefore or die, we are the Lord's*.[1] For himself he can say: *My earnest expectation and hope . . . is* that *Christ shall be magnified in my body, whether by life or by death*.[2] Every individual believer in the first age regarded himself as *the Lord's*, and this thought was the inspiration of a service that was 'perfect freedom'; even the Christian slave could account himself *the Lord's freedman*, since he *served the Lord Christ*.[3]

But it is of a corporate rather than an individual relation that S. Paul speaks, when he compares the Headship of Christ to the husband's authority over the wife; for the Spouse of Christ is not in the New Testament the soul, as in later Christian thought, but the Church.[4] Further, His Church in this connexion is the whole congregation of baptized believers, not the particular community of Christians 'sojourning' at Ephesus or Laodicea, Corinth or Rome;[5] nor again the aggregate of such local churches; nor is it a conception originating in 'an expansion or extension

---

[1] Rom. xiv. 7 f.   [2] Phil. i. 20.

[3] 1 Cor. vii. 22 ἀπελεύθερος Κυρίου, Col. iii. 24.

[4] Cf. Jo. iii. 29, Apoc. xix. 7, xxi. 2, 9, xxii. 17.

[5] In 2 Cor. xi. 2 it is the local Church which is 'espoused'; in Ephesians, the universal Church is in view.

of the thought of each local Ecclesia,'[1] nor a heavenly Ecclesia which does not consist of men on earth; but the whole number of Christ's baptized members on earth, regarded as a visible unity.[2] It is this great oecumenical society, the 'Holy Church' of the earliest baptismal creed, the 'Holy Catholic and Apostolic Church' of somewhat later forms, which can claim the Ascended Christ as its Head. Although a visible body, living on earth under visible officers, and offering a visible worship, its Head is invisible, and its relations with Him are purely spiritual. On the part of the Head they are maintained through the Holy Spirit, by whom as Christ's Vicar on earth 'the whole body of the Church is governed and sanctified.' On the part of the Body, the Headship of Christ is recognized by loyalty to His authority in all things. The Lord's instructions to the first missionaries of the Gospel required them not only to evangelize and baptize the nations,[3] but also to teach those whom they baptized to observe all that He had enjoined upon themselves (ὅσα ἐνετειλάμην ὑμῖν). But the loyalty which the Church owes to Christ cannot be restricted to the observance of injunctions delivered during His life on earth. There are few

[1] Cf. Hort, *Ecclesia*, p. 147 f.

[2] Hort, *ibid.*: 'it is a serious misunderstanding of these Epistles [Eph., Col.] to suppose, as is sometimes done, that the Ecclesia here spoken of is an Ecclesia wholly in the heavens, not formed of human beings.'

[3] Mt. xxviii. 19 f.

THE HEAD

express commandments left by Christ, beyond the observance of the Sacraments; the new law is a law of love, in the spirit and not in the letter. To obey the law of love, however, to follow the religion of the Spirit, is in fact a far severer test of loyalty than the keeping of any code of external laws. The Church shews her subjection to Christ in that world-long endeavour to conform life to the mind of Christ which, amid many shortcomings, characterizes all sincere Christians; in the *gesta Christi* which in all ages have followed the extension of the Gospel, even when the faith that was preached has been defective or corrupt, or the methods employed to propagate it have departed widely from those of the Apostolic age.

It may be asked whether the spiritual Headship of Christ can find visible expression on earth. More than one attempt has been made in the history of the Church to answer this question in the affirmative. The Western Church has had its human 'Vicar of Christ'; in our own country the revolt from the Papacy produced a 'Supreme Head.' But it must be admitted that neither Papalism nor Anglican Erastianism has borne such fruits as to encourage the belief that it is good for the Church to be under a visible Head, whether priestly or monarchical. Even if such an institution be not in theory incompatible with the spiritual Headship of Christ, in practice it certainly tends to obscure and thrust the latter aside. In a national Church the supremacy of the sovereign over all persons and in all causes within his dominions may be inevitable, and perhaps need not interfere with the spiritual independence of the Body of Christ, though it must be confessed that it often seems to do so. In the universal Church the Episcopate possesses a constitutional authority which we believe to be according to the mind of Christ, who Himself gave pastors and teachers, helps and governments. But we give neither to Bishop nor King the Headship which Christ has reserved for Himself. The erection of any human authority into a spiritual autocracy comes too perilously near to the assumption of rights and powers which belong to the Supreme *Pastor and Bishop of* all Christian *souls.*

2. But the thought of Christ as the Head of the Church suggests to S. Paul another line of thought which is even more fruitful. He is not only the dominating, directing Power which the Body obeys and follows, but the source of its vitality and of its vital energies.

The comparison of the Church to the human body first appears in the first Epistle to the Corinthians.[1] There it is worked out at some length, but without reference to the head as an organ; and, though hand

[1] 1 Cor. xii. 12 ff.

THE HEAD

and foot, ear and eye and nostrils, parts comely and uncomely, are specified, the crown and glory of the whole body is passed in silence. Moreover, it is the local Christian body which the Apostle has in view and not the whole congregation of the faithful throughout the world; *ye*, the Apostle says, *i.e.* you, Corinthian believers, *are the Body of Christ, and severally members thereof.* In Romans, written from Corinth two or three years later, the same metaphor is again used with similar restrictions. But in Ephesians and Colossians, the fruit of the undisturbed leisure and riper thought of the two years' imprisonment at Rome, the Body of Christ is seen to be a worldwide society, and its relation to Christ to be organically such as that of the human body to the head. The first of these points may have been suggested to S. Paul's mind by his enforced stay in the centre of the Empire; 'the unity which comprehended both Jew and Gentile under the bond of subjection to the Emperor of Rome,'[1] pointed to 'the truer unity which bound together in one society all believers in the Crucified Lord.' It was this great spiritual unity which, as S. Paul now saw, was in the fullest sense the Body of Christ; and Christ stood in the same relation to it as the head to the members of the body. When the Apostle came to think of the functions of the brain he found that they

[1] Hort, *Ecclesia*, p. 144.

presented a striking analogy to the functions which the Ascended Christ fulfils towards the Universal Church. What these are we learn from two passages in these Epistles which may be placed in parallel columns for the convenience of comparison.

The Head, even Christ, from whom all the Body, being fitly framed and knit together (συναρμολογούμενον καὶ συνβιβαζόμενον) *through every ligament of the supply* (διὰ πάσης ἁφῆς τῆς ἐπιχορηγίας), *according to the working in the measure of each several part, maketh increase of the body unto the building up of itself in love.*

The Head, from whom all the Body, being supplied and knit together (ἐπιχορηγούμενον καὶ συνβιβαζόμενον) *through the ligaments and bands* (διὰ τῶν ἁφῶν καὶ συνδέσμων),[1] *increaseth with the increase of God.*[2]

'The Apostle is using,' as the Dean of Westminster points out, 'the physiological terms of the Greek medical writers, and we can almost see him turn to the beloved physician... before venturing to speak in technical language of "every ligament of the whole apparatus" of the human frame.'[3] 'In both places,' he adds, 'the function assigned to the ἁφαί is that of holding the body together in the unity

---

[1] On ἁφή and σύνδεσμος see Lightfoot on Col. ii. 19, comparing Robinson on Eph. iv. 16.

[2] Eph. iv. 15 f., Col. ii. 19.

[3] *Ephesians*, p. 104.

which is necessary to growth.'[1] But in both the unity and the growth of the body are regarded as dependent on the head, the ligaments being only the means by which the body is kept in communication with the brain. Of the two passages, the shorter, which was perhaps the first to be written, represents this dependence more clearly. The Colossians are warned against cutting themselves off from the Christ through the cult of angels, and thus losing the vital energy which can permeate the members of the Body only when they are in union with the Head. In Ephesians the Apostle's purpose is somewhat different, as may be seen by glancing at the context (iv. 7 ff.). Each believer, he teaches, has received from the Ascended Christ his own measure of grace. It is the Ascended Christ who has given the Church Apostles, Prophets, Evangelists, Pastors and Teachers, to prepare the Saints for a life of service, and thus to build the edifice of the Christian Body, with the ultimate purpose of bringing all to the maturity, the spiritual stature, the fulness of life, which characterizes the completed Christ. For it is this at which, in the face of many difficulties and perils, we must steadily aim—to grow up in all things into conformity with our Head. From Him comes the principle of growth in the Body, working through the means of union which connect us with Him in His ascended life, and

[1] *Ephesians*, p. 186.

operative in each individual member according as he partakes of the Head's vital power.

As often in S. Paul, especially in the chief Epistles of the Roman captivity, the thought is too great for the words. But the general sense is clear. The Head of the Ecclesia is in heaven; but although invisible, He is in the closest union with His Body, which is on earth. There is a great system of communications between Christ and the Church, which makes Head and members a living unity. Upon the use of this system depends the life or growth of each member, and the ultimate maturity of the whole Body. For the Church is still immature; it has not come to 'perfectness of age in Christ.' The Head has been perfected through suffering; the perfecting of the members of the Body must be reached through union with the Head. This is the teaching of the Vine and the Branches under another figure; neither the branches apart from ($\chi\omega\rho\iota\varsigma$) the vine, nor the members apart from the head can thrive or even live. But Nature has provided for vital communication between root and branches, head and members; and in the higher nature of the Christian life there is a similar provision. The knitting and fitting together of men in the unity of the Church goes forward through successive generations, and wherever men are thus vitally united to Christ in His Church, the life of Christ flows into them, and the process of spiritual growth goes forward. As each generation is gathered into the unseen world, the time draws nearer when the Body of Christ will be complete, and its maturity revealed in the perfect life.

A fine note in Bishop Lightfoot's commentary on Colossians[1] points out how modern knowledge, so far from wrecking S. Paul's analogy, has given to it fresh force and meaning. 'Any exposition of the nervous system more especially reads like a commentary on his image of the relations between the body and the head.... The volition communicated from the brain to the limbs, the sensations of the extremities telegraphed back to the brain, the absolute mutual sympathy between the head and the members, the instantaneous paralysis ensuing on the interruption of continuity, all these add to the completeness and life of the image.'

If it be asked what are the ligaments or bands by which we are united to Christ our Head and receive of His fulness, S. Paul's silence on this point may be taken for a warning that no very precise, certainly no exhaustive, answer can be given. The two great Sacraments must undoubtedly hold a first place among them, for in S. Paul's system Baptism is the initial rite of corporate union with Christ, and the Eucharistic Bread is the communion of the Body of Christ, by which we are preserved in the unity of the Church.[2]

[1] *Colossians* [1875], p. 266. [2] 1 Cor. xii. 13, Gal. iii. 27, 1 Cor. x. 16 f.

Other sacramental rites, such as the laying on of hands upon the baptized for imparting the fuller gifts of the Holy Spirit, may also claim a place. But all means of grace—prayer, the word of God, devout meditation, spiritual communion, all religious acts by which the human spirit lays hold on things eternal—seem to come within the range of the Apostle's thought. Yet we know far too little of the secrets of our spiritual life, too little also of the wealth of Christ's power of drawing men to Himself, to dogmatize on such a point. It is enough to be sure that means of union with Christ exist in abundance within the Body of the Church, of which we are members.

In one respect the analogy of the human body fails us. The ligaments and bands of the physical system work automatically; our means of communication with the Ascended Christ are inoperative without the concurrence of the individual will. Men work out their own salvation, although, and even because, it is God that worketh in them both the will to work and the work itself in all its stages.[1] Thus the Christ lives in His members so far as they abide in Him, dwelling in their hearts by His Spirit, as they dwell in Him by their faith.[2] The same process goes forward corporately in the whole Body

---

[1] Phil. ii. 13 θεὸς γάρ ἐστιν ὁ ἐνεργῶν καὶ τὸ θέλειν καὶ τὸ ἐνεργεῖν.
[2] John xv. 3, Eph. iii. 17.

THE HEAD

of the Church. The Church lives and grows as it reciprocates the action of the Head, suffering loss of strength and vitality whenever it fails to respond to His Spirit. Ecclesiastical history is a running comment on this text. It shews periods of spiritual growth, and periods of decline, of torpor, and almost of death;[1] and the former often synchronize with times of persecution and social loss, whilst the latter are found in times of outward prosperity. In days of storm and stress the Church has realized her fellowship with her Head, and dependence on Him; whereas in good days she has said to herself, I *have need of nothing*, and has forgotten that apart from Him she is spiritually helpless—*miserable and poor and blind and naked.*[2]

There is another side to this dependence of the Body on the Head, which is not to be overlooked. S. Paul does not hesitate to represent the Head as on His part depending upon the members for the full realization of His office and work. As the head cannot fulfil its functions apart from the body, so the Christ is incomplete without His Church. Thus, in the Apostle's startling words, the Church is *the fulness* (τὸ πλήρωμα) *of him who is being fulfilled all in all*—for so the best interpreters, ancient and modern, bid us trans-

---

[1] Apoc. iii. 1 νεκρὸς εἶ, iii. 15 χλιαρὸς εἶ.
[2] Apoc. iii. 17.

late.¹ The Ascended Christ still needed, and still needs, to fulfil Himself in the life of His Body, the Church: 'the work which He came to do on earth was not completed when He passed from the sight of men ... part by part He was ... fulfilled in the community of His disciples.'² The idea of the Christ is incomplete without the Church; as the ages pass on and the Church approaches her consummation, the Christ attains the fulness of His life. We are already *complete in him*;³ He will in that day at length be complete in us. Meanwhile, He is relatively imperfect, so long as His Body has further growth to make. Even the Lord's sufferings are in this sense incomplete, for the sufferings of the Church belong to the predestined sum of those which the Christ must bear. *The cup that I drink, ye shall drink*,⁴ was His answer to the two who sought the highest honours of His Kingdom; and until that cup has been drained by the last Christian sufferer, the afflictions of the Christ are not made up. S. Paul, therefore, dares to say that he himself was helping to reduce this shortage: *I fill up on my part the deficiencies* (ἀνταναπληρῶ τὰ ὑστερή-ματα) *of the afflictions of the Christ, on behalf of his*

---

[1] Eph. i. 23 τὸ πλήρωμα τοῦ πάντα ἐν πᾶσιν πληρουμένου : see Westcott and Robinson, *ad loc.*, and Hort, *Ecclesia*, p. 147 f.

[2] Hort, *l.c.*   [3] Col. ii. 9 ἐστὲ πεπληρωμένοι ἐν αὐτῷ.

[4] Mc. x. 39.

THE HEAD

Body, that is the Church.[1] Deficiencies in the personal sufferings of Christ there are none, nor in their atoning worth; deficiencies in the sufferings which belong to the mystical Christ there were in S. Paul's time, and still are. Christ still suffers in His Body; He hungers and thirsts, is homeless and naked, is sick or in prison, when any of His members is in such a case.[2] It is the privilege of the needy, the toiling, the afflicted in mind, body, or estate, not only to find the power of the exalted Christ made perfect in their weakness, but to know that by that very weakness they bear their part in filling up the measure of His sufferings.[3]

Nor is this a theological fiction; there lies behind the words a great spiritual fact, which belongs to the economy of the ascended life—the active sympathy of the Head with the members of the Body. S. Paul speaks more than once of the sympathy of the members with each other: *whether one member suffereth, all the members suffer with it; or one member is honoured, all the members rejoice with it. Rejoice with them that rejoice; weep with them that weep.*[4] But it was reserved for the author of Hebrews to recognize that the Head has the same fellowship with the members as the members with one another. He does not, indeed, speak of Christ as the Head, but as the High

[1] Col. i. 24.
[2] Mt. xxv. 35 ff.
[3] 2 Cor. xii. 9.
[4] 1 Cor. xii. 26, Rom. xii. 15.

Priest; yet he directs attention to the human nature which is the ground of the sympathy with men which qualifies Him alike for the functions of High Priest and for those of Head. *We have not a High Priest that cannot be touched with the feeling of our infirmities* (συνπαθῆσαι ταῖς ἀσθενείαις ἡμῶν), *but one that hath been in all points tempted like as we are*;[1] and the same is true of our Head, seeing that High Priest and Head are one.

The human sympathy which in Jesus Christ joins hands with Divine compassion is a religious force by which the Gospel is distinguished from other monotheistic religions. The Old Testament has much to say of the *compassions* of Jahveh; they *fail not,* they *are new every morning.*[2] In Islam 'compassionate' is a stereotyped title of Allah.[3] But Christianity alone appeals to a Divine-human sympathy; only the Church can pray, 'By thy Fasting and Temptation, by thine Agony and Bloody Sweat, by thy Cross and Passion, by thy precious Death and Burial... in all time of our tribulation... in the hour of death and in the day of judgement, Good Lord, deliver us.' The sympathy of Christ is, we may be certain, attracted by all tempted and suffering humanity; but it finds a special outflow towards the members of

[1] Heb. iv. 15. [2] Lam. iii. 22 f.
[3] Thus *e.g.* the *Guide to Happiness*, a popular Mohammedan prayer-book, begins: "In the Name of God, the Compassionate, the Merciful."

His own Body. As when He was on earth His sympathy with sufferers could become operative only when their faith opened the door to His healing power, so it doubtless is now that He is in heaven; His will to relieve is conditioned by the response which is made to His sympathy. But within His Body His fellow-feeling has a free course; His ability to *succour those who are tempted* finds scope for constant exercise; and, as His members draw near to the throne of grace, they *receive mercy and find grace to help in time of need.*

If the Head is in effective sympathy with the Body, His sympathy is reciprocated by all His true members. The sympathy of the Church with the past suffering of her Head is expressed, year by year, in the solemnities of Lent and Holy Week; that she rejoices in His present joy is shewn at the great festivals of Easter and Ascension. The burst of light and colour which floods our churches at Easter and Ascensiontide, the festive services and glorious hymns of the Great Forty days, bear witness to the joy which thrills all Christian hearts that realize the resurrection and the exaltation of our Lord. The disciples who witnessed the Ascension *returned to Jerusalem with great joy, and were continually in the temple, blessing God.*[1] Sympathy with their Head sent a flood of joy coursing through their lives, even

[1] Lc. xxiv. 52 f.

when they were fresh from the last parting with Him, and the Holy Spirit, the other Comforter, had not yet come. To us the Spirit has revealed the glory of the Ascended Christ, and the stones might well cry out if, on our parts, there were no answer of exultation at the crowning of our Head.

VI.

THE MEDIATOR, INTERCESSOR, AND ADVOCATE.

1. THE Old Testament had a Mediator in the person of Moses. The Law *was ordained through Angels in the hands of a mediator*.[1] That angels were employed at the giving of the Law was a constant tradition of the Rabbis, based on Deut. xxxiii. 2, *He came from ten thousands of holy ones*.[2] But it was from Moses, a man of like passions with themselves, that Israel actually received the Law; the whole transaction was mediated by him. Nor was the Lawgiving the only occasion on which Moses came between God and His people. He is represented as the intermediary in all Divine communications with Israel, not as a mere prophet, but as one to whom God spoke *mouth to mouth, even manifestly and not in dark speeches*.[3] Similarly, on occasions of national

---

[1] Gal. iii. 19: see Lightfoot, *ad loc.*
[2] LXX σὺν μυριάσιν Κάδης, ἐκ δεξιῶν αὐτοῦ ἄγγελοι μετ' αὐτοῦ. Cf. Driver, *ad loc.*
[3] Exod. xxxiii. 11, Num. xii. 6 ff.

sin or peril, it is Moses who intercedes with God, and at his entreaty Jahveh 'repents.'[1] It was, however, the primary mediation at Sinai which impressed the Hebrew mind most deeply: the occasion on which Moses stood between the Lord and Israel on the holy mount, and God spoke to him out of the midst of the fire and gave him the Ten Words. To the intervention of Moses at that moment the nation owed the Covenant with God that distinguished Israel from the rest of the nations of the world. No wonder that from Philo[2] onwards the title of mediator was given by Jewish writers with one consent to the man who had represented the Hebrew people before God on that greatest day of their national life.

The New Testament does not deny the mediatorial character of Moses. *The Law was given by Moses.* But it places in sharp contrast with him another Mediator, who has won not for Israel only but for the world[3] a greater gift: *grace and truth came by Jesus Christ.* He is (*a*) *mediator of a better Covenant,*[4] *which has been enacted upon better promises*; He is also (*b*) the *one mediator between God and men.*[5]

---

[1] Exod. xxxii. 11 ff., 31 ff.
[2] *vit. Moys.* iii. 19 οἷα μεσίτης καὶ διαλλακτής.
[3] Jo. i. 17. For another point of contrast see Heb. iii. 3 ff.
[4] Heb. viii. 6.   [5] 1 Tim. ii. 5.

(a) It is the first of these views of the mediation of Christ which is in the mind of the author of Hebrews. The prophets had spoken of *a new covenant* which Jahveh would *make ... with the House of Israel and with the House of Judah*[1] at a future day. But the promise of a new covenant implies the supersession of the first, and the appointment of a new mediator to take the place of the mediator of the Law.[2] Under the new covenant the mediator is the High Priest; those two great offices, which under the Law were represented separately by Moses and Aaron, are both held by the Ascended Christ.

The conception of the Gospel as a new covenant in antithesis to the Law had found a place in the Epistles of S. Paul,[3] and in our Lord's words at the giving of the Eucharistic Cup—*This is my blood of the Covenant*, or *This Cup is the New Covenant in my blood.*[4] In both forms of the words reference is doubtless made to the scene in Exodus xxiv., where after the Lawgiving Moses, as mediator of the Law, first reads the Book of the Covenant in the hearing of Israel and receives their promise of obedience, and then sprinkles the Book and the people with sacrificial blood, by way of ratifying the contract between God and the congregation.[5] Even so our Mediator ratifies the New

---

[1] Jer. xxxi. 31 ff.   [2] Cf. Heb. viii. 7 f., 13.   [3] 2 Cor. iii. 6.
[4] Mc. xiv. 24 = Mt. xxvi. 28. 1 Cor. xi. 25, Lc. xxii. 20.
[5] Exod. xxiv. 6-8; cf. Heb. ix. 18 ff.

Covenant by the Cup of blessing, which He identifies with His own blood shed for the remission of sins.

Our Lord, then, is Mediator of the Covenant of the Gospel, with its better promises of forgiveness and grace, and its better sacrifice, the Sacrifice of Himself. His mediation, based on that one Sacrifice once offered upon earth, is carried forward within the veil, whither as High Priest He has gone to present it before God. On earth He still gives day by day in His Church the blood of the Covenant in the Eucharistic Cup, and the whole ministry of reconciliation,[1] committed by Him through His Church to the bishops and presbyters of Christendom, is an application of His Sacrifice to the wounds of fallen humanity. But behind all this, and the sole cause of its efficacy, is the direct mediation in heaven, where the One Mediator stands between God and men. The Church needs and can have none other. We *are come ... to Jesus, the mediator of a new covenant, and to the blood of sprinkling* that cries for mercy and grace.[2]

(*b*) In one of his latest letters S. Paul points out that the mediation of our Lord is, further, a mediation on behalf of the whole race. He exhorts that *supplications, prayers, intercessions, thanksgivings, be made for all men*, including *kings and all that are in high place*, the heathen emperors and their subor-

---

[1] 2 Cor. v. 18 f.   [2] Heb. xii. 22, 24.

dinates. *God our Saviour*, he adds, *willeth that all men should be saved, and come to the knowledge of the truth. For there is one God, one mediator also between God and men, himself man, Christ Jesus, who gave himself a ransom for all.*[1] The argument is clear: God, who is the Saviour of believers, wills also the salvation of the world; the One God is the God of the whole human race, and desires the good of all He has made. In like manner the One Mediator represents all mankind; He took their common nature, and He offered Himself in that nature for all. Therefore the Church can pray for all men, and all men can partake of the common salvation through the sacrifice and mediation of Jesus Christ.[2]

We are reminded of the only passage in the Old Testament where the word 'mediator' ($\mu\epsilon\sigma\iota\tau\eta s$) is found in the Greek Bible. Job is complaining of the vast disadvantage under which he seems to labour when he, a mortal man, draws near to the Infinite:

He is not a man, as I am, that I should answer him,
  That we should come together in judgement;
There is no daysman[3] *betwixt us,*
  That might lay his hand upon us both.[4]

---

[1] 1 Tim. ii. 1 ff.
[2] Cf. 1 John ii. 2, where the same truth is taught in other words.
[3] Heb. מוֹכִיחַ, LXX, $\mu\epsilon\sigma\iota\tau\eta s$: an umpire, arbiter, mediator (cf. xvi. 21).
[4] Job ix. 33.

Job is confronted by the greatest problem that perplexed ancient thinkers: how the insurmountable distance between God and man is to be spanned. But the question is not with him an intellectual puzzle, as it was with Philo the Alexandrian, and with the Gnostic teachers who came after Philo, but a personal concern. Brought face to face with God, the soul of the sufferer finds itself helpless to plead its cause with Infinite Power; feels that it can only submit and endure; is conscious of the need of a 'daysman,' *i.e.* an umpire who can lay one hand on God and one on man, and claim to mediate between them. Such a Mediator, S. Paul teaches, has now been appointed in the person of the exalted Christ. Of His relation to God the Apostle has spoken abundantly elsewhere, and he assumes it here. His relation to ourselves is emphasized by the one word 'man'—not 'the man,' as in the Authorized Version, nor 'a man,' but simply 'man'[1]—possessing our common human nature, and therefore capable of representing humanity, and, as the divinely appointed Mediator, standing between God and all mankind. Man sits in Jesus Christ on the Throne of God, and in Him the race has a 'daysman' betwixt itself and God who can 'lay his hand on both.' Thus the distance between the Infinite and the finite is bridged over by the Incarnation and the Ascension.

[1] Ἰησοῦς Χριστός, ἄνθρωπος.

But the incarnate and ascended Lord is also *the Lamb of God which taketh away the sin of the world*,[1] and therefore can mediate not only between the finite and the Infinite, but between sinners and the All-holy. Jesus Christ is not only man, but also the *Ransom for all* men, and He has ascended that He may present His Sacrifice. No obstacle remains in the way of those who come to God by Him.

2. The One Mediator is also Intercessor and Advocate. (*a*) Intercession goes a step further than mediation. A mediator may feel that he has done his work when he has introduced the two parties who are at issue with each other, and prepared the way for a discussion of their differences, leaving it to the parties themselves to settle the matter as they can. But an intercessor (ὁ ἐντυγχάνων) does not stop with simple mediation. He is one who uses his opportunity of saying a word on behalf of the person in whose interests he intervenes. If his word or his arguments have weight, this is of course a very important addition to the service which he has rendered by bringing the man face to face with the other party; it may turn the scale in his favour; whereas without it mediation might have been either abortive or even disastrous in its effects. Now our Lord's mediation passes into intercession in the case

[1] Jo. i. 29.

of all who come to God by Him. *Who shall lay anything to the charge of God's elect?* ... *It is Christ Jesus that died, yea rather, that was raised from the dead, who is at the right hand of God, who also maketh intercession for us* (ὃς καὶ ἐντυγχάνει ὑπὲρ ἡμῶν).[1] The 'intercession' of Christ is here made, as will be seen, the very climax of His saving activities: death, resurrection, exaltation to the right hand, all culminate in this. Our hope does not rest on a dead Christ, but on one who is *alive for evermore*; nor again on a Christ who merely lives, but on one who lives and reigns with God; nor, once more, simply on the fact of His exaltation, but on the knowledge that this exalted Person uses His opportunity to lay our case before God. The Rabbis spoke of Israel having both an Accuser and a Defender[2] in the Court of heaven. But *the Accuser of the brethren*, or of *the Israel of God*, as St. Paul would say, lays charges against them in vain, since they have the Ascended Christ to speak on their behalf.

The other passage in the New Testament which speaks of our Lord as Intercessor is even more instructive. He *hath his priesthood unchangeable; wherefore also he is able to save to the uttermost them*

---

[1] Rom. viii. 33 f.
[2] Satan or Sammael (the κατήγορος), and Michael (the συνήγορος); cf. Dan. xii. 1, Apoc. xii. 7 ff.

MEDIATOR, INTERCESSOR, ADVOCATE

that draw near to God through him, seeing he ever liveth to make intercession (εἰς τὸ ἐντυγχάνειν) *for them.*[1] The intercession of Christ depends upon His priesthood, and since He is a priest for ever, His intercession also is permanent. He can therefore carry on to its completion (εἰς τὸ παντελές) every case that He undertakes to defend, and thus is able to guarantee to those who approach God through His mediation entire restoration to the Divine favour and blessing. Nay, to do this is the very purpose of His life in heaven; He ever lives for this end, that He may intercede with God on their behalf. There can be no suspension of His intercessory work so long as the world lasts. He lives to intercede, and intercedes by the very fact of his High-priestly life.

For the intercession of the Ascended Christ is not a prayer, but a life. The New Testament does not represent Him as an *orante*, standing ever before the Father, and with outstretched arms, like the figures in the mosaics of the catacombs, and with strong crying and tears pleading our cause in the presence of a reluctant God; but as a throned Priest-King, asking what He will from a Father who always hears and grants His request. Our Lord's life in heaven is His prayer. But in the days of His flesh He prayed as we pray, and one of His prayers of intercession[2] remains to help the Church to realize

[1] Heb. vii. 24.   [2] Jo. xvii. 1 ff.

in some measure the ends which He sets before Him in His intercessory life.

The Lord had spoken His last word of teaching and comfort to His disciples: *be of good cheer; I have overcome the world.*[1] Then He turned from men to God, His Father in heaven. He lifted up His eyes to heaven and prayed on that night before the Passion, first for Himself and then for His own. We learn, as the prayer proceeds, what it is that He asks for the Church, and what He does not ask. *Holy Father, keep them in thy name which thou hast given me, that they may be one, even as we are.... I pray not that thou shouldest take them from the world, but that thou shouldest keep them from the evil one.... Neither for these only do I pray, but for them also that believe on me through their word, that they may all be one.... Father, that which thou hast given me, I will that where I am, they also may be with me, that they may behold my glory which thou hast given me.*[2] The Lord, it will be seen, desires for His Church not segregation from the world, but safe-keeping from the evil power that works in it. He asks for her such present oneness of faith and love as may convince the world of the Divine mission of the Christ, and in the life to come the endless vision of the glory of God in the face of the Incarnate Son. Such, then, are the ends which our Lord's life in heaven has

[1] Jo. xvi. 33.   [2] Jo. xvii. 11, 15, 20, 24.

MEDIATOR, INTERCESSOR, ADVOCATE 97

in view. The words of prayer, which befitted Him on the eve of the Passion, have no place in His present state. But they witness to the general purpose to which His intercession is directed and which it must accomplish.

(b) Cognate to the title of Intercessor is that of Advocate or Paraclete. The word is used in the New Testament only by S. John, and applied by him to our Lord but twice, indirectly in his Gospel and expressly in his first Epistle. When Christ says, *The Father shall give you another Paraclete*,[1] it is implied that He Himself had been such. The Epistle adds that He is such still: *if any man sin, we have an Advocate ($\pi\alpha\rho\acute{\alpha}\kappa\lambda\eta\tau o\nu$) with the Father, Jesus Christ, who is righteous*.[2] An advocate or paraclete is in the most general sense of the word simply one who is called to the help of a man in any necessity or distress. It may be merely to administer comfort, or to give counsel or protection that he is summoned; and this was our Lord's relation to the Twelve during His life, and is the present relation of His Spirit to the Church. But Christ as our Advocate with the Father appears in a further light; His advocacy in heaven is concerned with the problem of sin. As Mediator He gains access for us into the presence of God; as Intercessor, He furthers our petitions; as Advocate, He meets

---

[1] Jo. xiv. 16. [2] 1 Jo. ii. 1.

the charge that lies against us on the score of sin. For believers the life of habitual sin is at an end, as S. John strongly insists elsewhere: *whosoever lives in sin* (πᾶς ὁ ἁμαρτάνων) *hath not seen* Christ, *neither knoweth him*.[1] But isolated acts of sin are possible in the holiest lives, and frequent in the lives of most of us; and on such occasions, whenever a Christian is conscious of having committed a sin (ἐάν τις ἁμαρτῇ), the advocacy of the Ascended Christ becomes of supreme importance to him. Three great facts give to His advocacy a force which assures the penitent who trusts to it of acceptance. He is *with the Father*, *i.e.* in the presence of God, and upon God's very Throne. He is *righteous*, He has as man fulfilled all righteousness; in Him, from His birth to His death, the Father was well pleased. And He is *the Propitiation for our sins*—not simply one who has made propitiation, but one who is Himself the Sacrifice, the *Lamb as it had been slain*, whose mere presence in heaven is an all-prevailing plea for the forgiveness of the sins of those whom He represents. He is also, S. John adds, the Propitiation *for the whole world*;[2] for the efficacy of His great offering is not limited to the Church. Even for the world the Propitiation pleads that it may have time for repentance: *Lord, let it alone this year also: Father,*

---

[1] 1 Jo. iii. 6.   [2] 1 Jo. ii. 2.

MEDIATOR, INTERCESSOR, ADVOCATE

forgive them, for they know not what they do.[1] But perhaps the advocacy of which S. John speaks is a more special and direct plea for pardon than the unbelieving world can expect: *I pray not for the world, but for those whom thou hast given me, for they are thine.*[2] The Mediator stands between God and all mankind; the Intercessor and Advocate represents before God the universal Church. Yet there is no limit to the love or power of the Ascended Christ; and no human being that approaches God through the One Mediator fails to engage the Intercessor and Advocate on his behalf.

The ancient collects of the Western Church remind us many times in our daily services that the whole fabric of Christian prayer rests on the heavenly intercession of our Lord. The words, 'through Jesus Christ our Lord,' or one of the many changes rung upon this theme, are so constantly upon our lips that they are apt to be regarded merely as a liturgical form, the traditional ending of our Church prayers. But the tradition embodies a vital truth and rests upon the words of Christ: *I go unto the Father*, the Lord said, *and whatsoever ye shall ask in my name, that will I do, that the Father may be glorified in the Son.... I chose you and appointed you ... that whatsoever ye shall ask of the Father in my name, he may give it you.* And afterwards: *Verily, verily, I say*

[1] Lc. xiii. 8; xxiii. 34.   [2] Jo. xvii. 9.

unto you, If ye shall ask anything of the Father, he will give it you in my name. Hitherto have ye asked nothing in my name; ask, and ye shall receive, that your joy may be fulfilled.[1] The words, *in my Name*, though they do not prescribe a formula, evidently express a new condition under which all requests must in future be made known to God. The fulness of joy is only for those who realize their relation to the ascended Lord, and consciously approach the Father through the ascended Son.

Our Lord is the One Mediator, the only way to the Father. Yet there is another Advocate, another Intercessor. While the Incarnate Son is our Advocate with the Father and makes intercession at the right hand of God, the Holy Spirit is our Advocate on earth, and makes intercession for us in the depths of our hearts.[2] So awful and blessed a thing is Christian prayer that no petition finds its way from man to God without the co-operation of two Divine Persons, one working with man on earth, the other for man in heaven. The Spirit inspires prayer, or the desire which can as yet find no full expression in words; and the Son presents it to the Father, and claims acceptance for it on the ground of His righteousness, His sacrifice, His exaltation of manhood to the Throne of God.

---

[1] Jo. xiv. 12 f., xv. 16, xvi. 23 f. [2] Rom. viii. 26 f.

VII.

THE FORERUNNER.

THE Ascended Head is the Forerunner of the Body. The separation which began at the Ascension cannot be permanent: *where I am*, the Lord promised, *there shall also my minister* (διάκονος) *be; if any man minister* (διακονῇ) *to me, him will the Father honour.*[1] The promise is repeated in another form in the last of the Apocalyptic messages to the Churches: *he that overcometh, I will give to him to sit down with me in my throne.*[2]

The title 'Forerunner' (πρόδρομος) is usually given to the Baptist, who went *before the face of the Lord to make ready his ways.*[3] The New Testament, however, uses the word but once, and then in reference to our Lord Himself. As the Baptist prepared the way of Christ, so the Ascended Christ prepares the way of His Church. It is to the author of Hebrews that we owe this view of the ascended life, as we

[1] Jo. xii. 26.   [2] Apoc. iii. 21.
[3] Lc. i. 76 (cf. 17).

owe to him so much else that assists us to form a true estimate of its importance. He likens *the hope set before us* to *an anchor of the soul,* seeing that it is *both sure and stedfast and entering into that which is within the veil; whither,* he adds, *as a forerunner Jesus entered for us, having become a high priest for ever after the order of Melchizedek.*[1] Like ships at anchor, the souls of the faithful, though tossed by the waves of life, have no cause to fear shipwreck, so long as their hope keeps a firm grip upon the realities of the unseen world. But this can only be done by those who bear in mind that the great High Priest of the Church has gone within the veil as the Forerunner of His brethren, that they may follow in due time.

In a sense the Church already follows her High Priest and Head. It is given to us already to 'ascend in heart and mind' to our Lord, and 'with Him continually dwell,' as the Ascension Day collect prays that we may. In the words of S. Paul, *God raised us up with* Christ, *and made us to sit with him in the heavenly places*;[2] we are sharers not only in the risen but the ascended life. Nor do we share by representation only; through Christ, as we have seen, we have the right of personal access to God, liberty to pass the veil and enter the Holiest (παρρησίαν εἰς τὴν εἴσοδον τῶν ἁγίων). To this

---
[1] Heb. vi. 18 ff.   [2] Eph. ii. 6.

THE FORERUNNER

extent the Head of the Body was immediately followed by the members, and the way into the Holiest has been open from the Apostolic age to our own.

But *the hope set before us* evidently goes further than this, for it contemplates heights that are above us yet. We do not *hope* for access to God through Christ in prayer and Communion; we have it, it is ours in this present life. But there is much more that is not yet ours, and it is for this that we wait and hope. We feel the chain tugging at the anchor, and we know that the anchor is *sure and stedfast* and firmly planted within the veil: we are conscious of the attractive power of the Ascended Lord. But meanwhile the higher world into which He has passed remains unexplored, even though our treasure and our heart are there. Some better thing is reserved[1] for us; there is to be an ascension, not of heart and mind only, but of the whole man, corresponding to the Ascension of Jesus Christ; an entrance into the Holiest not only in the way of prayer and the Sacraments, but of beatific vision and full satisfaction. The Forerunner will secure this also for His Church. The New Testament witnesses to future happy conditions of existence for which our present life in Christ is preparatory. And this highest hope of man stands connected with the

[1] 1 Pet. i. 4 τετηρημένην.

Ascension and the ascended life of our Lord. It is this great truth which the author of Hebrews so felicitously expresses when he gives to the ascended Head of the Church the title of Forerunner.

In a well-known passage of the fourth Gospel our Lord, without using the title, describes His own work as Prodromos. *In my Father's house are many mansions (μοναί); if it were not so, I would have told you; for I go to prepare a place for you. And if I go and prepare a place for you, I come again, and will receive (παραλήμψομαι) you unto myself; that where I am, there ye-may be also.*[1] The words are simplicity itself; yet as we read them we are perhaps conscious that it is the form only which is simple and not the thought. The hope which they inspire, in fact, transcends thought. But some points are clear. *My Father's House* (ἡ οἰκία τοῦ πατρός μου) is elsewhere in S. John our Lord's name for the Temple;[2] here it clearly is the immaterial, non-localized, Sanctuary of the Divine Presence, into which the humanity of Jesus was shortly to pass. In that Sanctuary there are *many mansions*,[3] as our Authorized Version translates, following the Vulgate, and followed by the Revisers of 1881. Yet neither the Greek word

---

[1] Jo. xiv. 2 ff.

[2] Jo. ii. 16 τὸν οἶκον τοῦ πατρός μου. Cf. Lc. ii. 49 ἐν τοῖς τοῦ πατρός μου.

[3] μοναὶ πολλαί, *multae mansiones*. Cf. Exod. xvii. 1, Num. xxxiii. 1.

nor the Vulgate Latin equivalent meant what the English word means in its common acceptation—a 'great house,' or even what the etymology might suggest, a permanent abode. They speak rather of 'resting-places,' havens of refreshment, to be found here and there along the road that leads to God; and if so, as Bishop Westcott remarks, 'repose and progress are combined in the vision of the future.'[1] Or it may be that the 'mansions of the Father's house' are intended to recall the chambers of the Temple-courts, used by the priests in attendance and for other purposes.[2] The great Sanctuary of the eternal world is represented as possessing an abundance of such chambers for the use of those who wait upon the heavenly altar. But whichever of these pictures was in the mind of our Lord, or of the writer of the Gospel, the general meaning is clear; in that world where He has gone, there is room and to spare for all His followers. They will find no lack of resting-places after the journey of life, from whence, when they are refreshed, a new start can be made towards the final goal; abodes await them within the walls of the courts of the Lord's House, where they will evermore be near to the altar and the Sanctuary, going out thence no more.[3] Christ is gone to the Father's House to

[1] *S. John* (ed. 1908), ii. p. 167. [2] See *Enc. Bibl.* iv. col. 4946.
[3] Cf. Apoc. iii. 12 for another image.

make ready for the great host of the redeemed. When all is ready, He returns to receive them, not only to His Father's House, but to Himself, to intercourse and closest union with His ascended life.

All this was yet future on the night before the Passion, and it is future still; so far at least as we ourselves are concerned. How is it to be realized? When and how will the Ascended Christ receive us to Himself?

1. The New Testament seems to justify the belief that the individual soul, if faithful unto death, is received by our Lord at the moment of departure. As the Incarnate Son committed His human spirit into the hands of the Father,[1] so His first martyr, Stephen, committed his spirit to the Son.[2] The same belief is expressed in S. Paul's willingness *to be absent* (ἐκδημῆσαι) *from the body, and to be at home* (ἐνδημῆσαι) *with the Lord*,[3] and his later desire to break up his camp here (ἀναλῦσαι) and go to be with Christ— 'a very far better thing' (πολλῷ μᾶλλον κρεῖσσον);[4] perhaps also in S. John's vision[5] of the great multitude who are *before the throne of God and ... serve him day and night in his temple* (ναῷ), while He who sits on the Throne spreads His Holy Presence over them, like a heavenly Tent of Meeting (σκηνώσει

---

[1] Lc. xxiii. 46. [2] Acts vii. 59. [3] 2 Cor. v. 6 ff.
[4] Phil. i. 23. [5] Apoc. vii. 9 ff.

THE FORERUNNER

ἐπ' αὐτούς), *and the Lamb which is in the midst of the Throne*—the once crucified, now glorified Christ—*shall be their Shepherd*; and certainly in the words *Blessed are the dead which die in the Lord from henceforth, that they may rest from their labours; for their works follow with them.*[1] It seems then that in some true sense the dead in Christ are already with Him *in Paradise*; that is, in the state of the dead they are conscious of the presence of Christ, and find rest and joy in it. This is not to deny that there may be in the intermediate state, as many have thought, some process of purification corresponding to the needs of individual souls. Unless the moment of death brings a moral and spiritual change, which we have no reason to expect from it, there can be few Christians whom it will find ready for the full joy of their Lord. But it may well be that whatever is still necessary for the perfecting[2] of the Christian character will come from the purgative power of a closer fellowship with the Holy One. Meanwhile the soul has reached the first 'resting-place' on its way to God, the first 'chamber' prepared for it in His House; where it abides in the hands

---

[1] Apoc. xiv. 13.

[2] *Made perfect* in Heb. xii. 23 must be taken, as it seems, to refer to such relative maturity as the discipline of life has brought, rather than to absolute completeness. Τελειοῦν is used in Hebrews in various senses short of absolute 'perfection'; cf. *e.g.* Heb. ii. 10, v. 9, ix. 9, x. 14, xi. 40.

of Christ, undergoing such further happy discipline as its needs may require.

2. But however we may represent to ourselves the state into which our Lord comes at the hour of death to call the souls of the faithful, it is certain that He has another coming and another call, and other mansions into which He will receive the whole Church at the Parousia. The words, *I will receive you unto myself* may well find a first fulfilment in the welcome of the individual Christian spirit, but the paramount thought in them is surely the welcome which the whole perfected Body will find at the Resurrection. All the New Testament writers point to this as the crowning moment of human history—the moment when the new humanity will be glorified with its glorious Head. Even in the Gospels we hear the distant welcome, *Come, ye blessed of my Father, inherit the Kingdom prepared for you from the foundation of the world.*[1] In the Epistles it swells into the triumphant note of an assured hope: *I reckon that the sufferings of this present time are not worthy to be compared with the glory which shall be revealed to usward. For the earnest expectation of the creation waiteth for the revealing of the sons of God.*[2] Or again: *As we have borne the image of the earthy, we shall also bear the image of the Heavenly.*[3] ... *We wait for a Saviour, the Lord Jesus Christ,*

[1] Mt. xxv. 34.   [2] Rom. viii. 18 f.   [3] 1 Cor. xv. 49.

who shall fashion anew the body of our humiliation, that it may be conformed to the body of his glory....[1] *When Christ, who is our life, shall be manifested, then shall ye also with him be manifested in glory....*[2] *An inheritance incorruptible and undefiled and that fadeth not away, reserved in heaven for you who by the power of God are guarded through faith unto a salvation ready to be revealed at the last time....*[3] *It is not yet made manifest what we shall be. We know that if he shall be manifested, we shall be like him, for we shall see him even as he is.*[4] Lastly, in the Apocalypse this same hope becomes a vision;[5] we see *a new heaven and a new earth*; and *the Holy City, new Jerusalem, coming down out of heaven from God*, is described with an extravagance of language which the Seer knows to be all too poor to set forth the perfect life. He who would translate these glowing words into the sobriety of modern speech must allow for their Oriental richness of colouring. But he will entirely misinterpret the preachers and writers of the first age if, in his desire to drop the apocalyptic symbolism, he eliminates from his presentation of the primitive Gospel the glowing hope of a future life with Christ in heaven.

In my Father's House are many mansions ... I ... will receive you unto myself.[6] Little as we can

[1] Phil. iii. 20 f.   [2] Col. iii. 4.   [3] 1 Pet. i. 4 f.
[4] 1 Jo. iii. 2.   [5] Apoc. xxi. 1 ff.   [6] Jo. xiv. 2.

apprehend the ways in which this promise will fulfil itself, there are two aspects of the heavenly life which it clearly reveals. It will be life consciously spent in the Presence of God, and it will be life in fellowship with Christ.

(a) All life is in the Presence of God ; all creation is the Father's House. This was recognized by the prophets of the Old Testament: *thus saith the Lord, The heaven is my throne, and the earth is my footstool; what manner of house will ye build unto me?*[1] But if the fact is acknowledged on all hands, it is realized but by few, and by these imperfectly. It is the supreme struggle of faith to live *as seeing him who is invisible.*[2] Death removes the sense-barrier, and there is doubtless truth in the conviction which is widely prevalent that the soul after its departure from the body finds itself face to face with God, *i.e.* it becomes conscious of His presence as it never was conscious of it here. But the Christian hope of the Resurrection of the body opens the prospect of something higher—a vision of God vouchsafed to the whole being through faculties unknown to us now ; a vision permeating the whole life with a consciousness of Infinite Love and Light. The Church can use the words of Job in a sense of which the writer never dreamed : *in my flesh shall I see God, whom I shall see for myself, and mine eyes shall behold, and not another.*[3] If we add to this belief the

---

[1] Isa. lxvi. 1.   [2] Heb. xi. 27.   [3] Job xix. 26 f.

knowledge that such a constant sight of God as He is will be to a perfected and sinless humanity neither overpowering nor embarrassing—that it will impose no strain upon the mind or spirit, inspire no fear that *hath torment*, but on the contrary a peace and a joy which passes understanding, it is clear that the vision will be 'beatific' indeed, leaving no want unsatisfied, fulfilling in itself the highest destiny of the creature. *Fecisti nos ad te, et inquietum est cor nostrum donec requiescat in te*:[1] 'We were made for Thee, and our hearts find rest nowhere short of Thee.'

(*b*) It would seem as if nothing could increase the greatness of this hope. Yet there is more, for the Lord continues: I *will receive you unto myself, that where I am there ye may be also.*[2] The beatific vision of God is seen in the heavenly life through the glorified humanity of Jesus Christ. *No man hath seen God at any time.*[3] So S. John writes, thinking of the present life; S. Paul adds, *Nor can see*, having in view also that which is to come.[4] In both orders the revelation of the Father is made only in the Son, *who is the image of the Invisible God*;[5] here, through *the light of the gospel of the glory of Christ*;[6] there, through the direct manifestation of the glorified humanity. The fuller and permanent sight of God will come to *the saints in light* through the perpetual

[1] Aug. *Confess.* i. 1. [2] Jo. xiv. 3. [3] Jo. i. 18.
[4] 1 Tim. vi. 16. [5] Col. i. 15. [6] 2 Cor. iv. 4.

Presence, visible to the organs of the spiritual body, of the manifested Lord. *Father, I will*—so He prayed on the night before the Passion—*that where I am they also may be with me, that they may behold my glory which thou hast given me.*[1] He had said a little before, *Now, O Father, glorify thou me with thine own self*[2] *with the glory which I had with thee before the world was.* His disciples, then, are to see the Divine glory of the Father, which was the Father's eternal gift to the Son, revealed in the ascended, glorified Christ. But more than this, they are to see it by being *with* Christ (μετ' ἐμοῦ)—in company with Him, as in the high life of heaven He moves in their midst after a manner which recalls the old days of His ministry in Galilee and at Jerusalem.[3] In the visions of the Apocalypse this eternal presence of Christ in the midst of His Church comes often into view. *I will come in to him, and will sup with him and he with me.... The Lamb ... shall guide them unto fountains of waters of life.... These are they which follow the Lamb whithersoever he goeth.... The lamp of the New Jerusalem is the Lamb.... The throne of God and of the Lamb shall be therein.*[4]

---

[1] Jo. xvii. 24; cf. verse 5.

[2] παρὰ σεαυτῷ, *i.e.* 'in fellowship with thee' (Westcott).

[3] Cf. Jo. xv. 27 ἀπ' ἀρχῆς μετ' ἐμοῦ ἐστέ.

[4] Apoc. iii. 20, vii. 17, xiv. 4, xxi. 23, xxii. 8.

THE FORERUNNER

How does our Forerunner prepare a place for us in His Father's House, where He Himself now is?

It would seem from another saying of Christ as if preparation had been made by the Father Himself from eternity: *inherit the kingdom prepared for you from the foundation of the world*;[1] and this accords with all that the Epistles teach us as to the eternal purpose of God. If further preparation were needed in time, it was made by the Incarnation, the Sacrifice, the Resurrection of our Lord; as the *Te Deum* sings: 'When Thou hadst overcome the sharpness of death, Thou didst open the Kingdom of Heaven to all believers.' And if we look more closely at the words with which the last discourse begins, we see that our Lord does not prepare *mansions* for the elect, but a *place* for them therein. The mansions are already lining the courts of the Father's House, and they are many—as many as the *great multitude which no man can number* of souls that are passing through the Church on earth on their way to fill them. What, then, remains for the Ascended Christ to do? How does He prepare the way of His Church as its Forerunner to heaven? In the first place, His own entrance in the completeness of His humanity into the unseen world is preparatory to our entrance: where human nature has gone in the person of the Second Adam, human nature can go

[1] Mt. xxv. 34.

when it has been perfected in His brethren. And His presence in heaven keeps the way open until we are ready to follow. Moreover, the preparation of our nature for heaven is entirely dependent on His glorified person. Neither the Father's eternal purpose nor His own life and sufferings on earth are operative apart from the ascended life, which is the source of the sanctifying Spirit. On it turns the whole working out of the destiny of the Church in the world. Much, indeed, must be done before He can present the Church to Himself. Death and resurrection must intervene; *this corruptible must put on incorruption, and this mortal must put on immortality,* and—yet greater change—this sinful, sinlessness. The predestined course of history must run itself out; the *gospel of the Kingdom* must have been *preached in the whole world for a testimony unto all the nations,*[1] and the last generation of the baptized have taken its place in the Body of Christ. All these vast movements pertaining to the entrance of the Church upon her final inheritance belong to the sphere of our Lord's present activities, and in all and through all He is preparing a place for us with Himself. There is, indeed, a corresponding work belonging to ourselves as individuals, and to the Church in her successive generations: by strenuous Christian effort by self-discipline, by devout use of prayer and sacra-

[1] Mt. xxiv. 14.

THE FORERUNNER 115

ments, His Bride makes herself ready.[1] But the authority which controls the whole process, the Hand which guides it, the grace which animates and sustains, are all His who has gone to prepare a place for her. The Forerunner is also the Way by which, after long following, the whole Church will reach at last the Father's 'House.

[1] Apoc. xix. 7 ἡ γυνὴ αὐτοῦ ἡτοίμασεν ἑαυτήν.

VIII.

THE PRESENCE IN THE MIDST.

THE Ascended Christ, as we have seen, is in constant touch and full sympathy with His Body on earth; all the sufferings, physical and spiritual, of all her members are, in some way unknown to us, telegraphed to the Head. But there is more. While in heaven, He is at the same time with the Church on earth, occupying Himself with the concerns of every congregation of the faithful. Not only is He the Head and Forerunner of the Church, but a Presence immanent in her midst.

We begin with our Lord's own statement of this truth. *I say unto you, that if two of you shall agree on earth as touching anything that they shall ask, it shall be done for them of my Father which is in heaven. For where two or three are gathered together in my name, there am I in the midst of them.*[1] Even two or three Christians met for common prayer or Eucharist constitute for the time being an ecclesia,

[1] Mt. xviii. 19 f.

a congregation of Christ's flock,[1] and may claim the promise of His presence; in such an assembly He will make the third or the fourth.[2] Our Lord is clearly speaking of days subsequent to His earthly life. The building of the ecclesia was still in the future,[3] and there is nothing to shew that men met in His Name to pray during His ministry or until after the Ascension. So long as He was with His disciples from day to day, usually living in their midst, there was no occasion for such meetings, nor for the promise of His presence. The whole passage is evidently anticipatory of times when men would desire to see one of the days of the Son of Man and desire it in vain, and the presence which is guaranteed to the Church is intended to take the place of the visible Christ. This view is confirmed by another passage in S. Matthew's Gospel, where the promise of the Presence is made to the Church as a whole, to hold good to the end of the present dispensation: *Lo, I am with you all the days, even unto the consummation of the age* (ἐγὼ εἰμὶ μεθ' ὑμῶν πάσας τὰς ἡμέρας, ἕως τῆς συντελείας τοῦ αἰῶνος).[4]

1. We have our Lord's guarantee that He is present wherever Christian men meet in His Name.

---

[1] Tertullian, *pud.* 21: 'ecclesiam dominus in tribus posuit'; *cast.* 7: 'ubi tres ecclesia est.'

[2] Cf. Dan. iii. 25.   [3] Mt. xvi. 18 οἰκοδομήσω τὴν ἐκκλησίαν μου.

[4] Mt. xxviii. 20.

As if to impress this fact by a picture lesson which those who witnessed it could never forget, on the night after the Resurrection, while ten of the Apostles and their company were assembled within closed and barred doors, *Jesus came and stood in the midst.* This appearance was repeated on the eighth day: again the disciples were within, their number now completed by the return of Thomas, and again *Jesus cometh, the doors being shut, and stood in the midst.*[1] It was an experience which, under other conditions, was to repeat itself at the weekly Lord's Day assemblies of the Church as long as the world should last.

From the beginning, or almost from the beginning, the churches met on the weekly day of the Resurrection to break the bread which the Lord Himself had called His Body.[2] It was the one visible memorial of His bodily presence; it was also an appointed means of union and fellowship with Him. *The bread which we break, is it not a communion of the body of Christ?*[3] *He that eateth my flesh and drinketh my blood,* the Lord had said, *abideth in me, and I in him*;[4] and this was His own prescribed way of eating and drinking His flesh and blood, and thus retaining His presence in the inner life, and, by reciprocation, abiding in Him. At the Eucharist, then,

[1] Jo. xx. 19, 26.   [2] Acts xx. 7.
[3] 1 Cor. x. 16.   [4] Jo. vi. 56.

THE PRESENCE IN THE MIDST

if at any time, the Church must have felt that she might look for the fulfilment of Christ's promise to be *in the midst*, and the Eucharist, with or without the attendant Agapé, was from the first the great act of common worship in which all the baptized ordinarily took part, and with which were associated all the prayers and intercessions, the offerings and devotions of the congregation. It was in the Eucharistic service, and not, as with us, at Morning and Evening Prayer, that the ancient Church pleaded with Christ His own promise that where two or three are gathered together in His Name He would grant their requests.[1] Not that there is reason to doubt that the Lord is present at our daily Common Prayer; if in many churches the bell for Matins and Evensong brings together literally but two or three, yet His words have graciously provided for such paucity of worshippers. But the Eucharist, which brings the Gift of His Body and Blood, and which by His command the whole Church does in commemoration of Him, must ever be specially connected in Christian thought with His promised Presence in the midst.

In the Eucharist, as we have seen in an earlier chapter, we have a counterpart of our Lord's Self-

---

[1] The so-called *Prayer of S. Chrysostom* is the 'Prayer of the third Antiphon' at the beginning of the liturgy of S. Basil, which is still used at certain seasons by the Orthodox Church of the East.

presentation in heaven. It is also our nearest approach to the worship of heaven; the symbols of the Body and Blood correspond to the symbolic Figure of the *Lamb as it had been slain*, which is the centre of the heavenly adoration. In the midst of the Throne and of the Court of Heaven, the Seer saw the Lamb standing, and before Him there prostrated themselves the Living Creatures and the Elders, representing Nature and the Church; and presently an outer circle of ten thousand times ten thousand angels took up the shout of praise, and beyond them again were heard the voices of all creation saying, *Unto him that sitteth on the throne, and unto the Lamb, be the blessing and the honour and the glory and the dominion for ever and ever.*[1] In this universal adoration of the Lamb, this conglorification of the Incarnate, sacrificed, glorified Son with the Eternal Father, the Church joins, as she kneels before the earthly symbols of His Presence, worshipping not an absent Lord, but one who is really and indeed in the midst of His people. No adoration, of course, is intended or ought to be done to the symbols—it is not the symbolic Figure of the Lamb that all heaven worships—nor to any corporal or localized presence whatsoever;[2] the Real Presence is after the manner of the spiritual life into which the humanity of the

[1] Apoc. v. 6 ff.
[2] See the last rubric after the Order of Holy Communion.

THE PRESENCE IN THE MIDST

Lord has passed.[1] But where Christ is present, although His presence is not corporal, He is to be adored.[2] The Church of England recognizes this with special solemnity at the Eucharist, both in the *Tersanctus* and in the *Gloria in excelsis*, which last she has removed to the end of the liturgy,[3] as if to make the adoration of the Ascended Christ the crowning act of her Eucharistic sacrifice. 'Thou that sittest at the right hand of God the Father, have mercy upon us. For thou only art holy; thou only art the Lord; thou only, O Christ, with the Holy Ghost, art most high in the glory of God the Father.' No words in the celestial liturgy of the Apocalypse rise above these, in which, Sunday by Sunday, we adore the Presence in our midst.

2. The vision with which the Apocalypse opens [4]

---

[1] Hooker's phrases (*E.P.* v. lv. 9), 'a presence of force and efficiency,' 'infinite in possibility of application,' seem not to recognize fully the powers of the risen and ascended Body of the Lord. On this see Gore, *Body of Christ*, p. 124 ff.

[2] St. Ambrose, *de Spir. s.* iii. 11, § 79, writes: 'caro Christi quam hodieque in mysteriis adoramus,' and S. Augustine, *enarr. in Ps.* xcvii.: "nemo autem illam carnem manducat nisi prius adoraverit." In both passages *caro Christi* is the Sacred Humanity, which is adorable because of its hypostatic union with the Word. No one eats the flesh of Christ in the Eucharist to his soul's health, in the sense of Jo. vi. 56 f., who has not first learnt to adore Christ as the God-Man.

[3] In the mediaeval office the *Gloria* stood before the Collect, Epistle, and Gospel.

[4] Apoc. i. 10 ff.

represents the Ascended Christ as in the midst of His Church for other and larger purposes than those of granting prayer and receiving adoration. He appears as the great Bishop of souls, inspecting the condition of local churches, and commending or censuring, rewarding or chastizing, as need may require. It is not a vision of the Lord as He was seen in the days of His flesh, nor as He appeared after His resurrection, but of the glorified Christ as He now is. The Figure is a symbolical representation of His present power and functions, which defies the skill of the artist to depict it upon canvas or paper, but expresses, after the manner of apocalyptic prophecy, the deathless life and the unspeakable majesty of the Ascended Lord. On the whole, the form is human—*like a son of man,* as the Seer guardedly says—but there are features which are not human as we know humanity: the snow-white head and hair, coupled with the strength of an ageless life, the eyes flashing like fire, the feet glowing like metal just taken from the furnace, the right hand bearing in the open palm a wreath of stars; while from the mouth there issues a sharp sword, and the face is like the midday sun of the Levant, and the voice as the roar of a cataract. It is a vision of glorified, deified, humanity. But it is not, as some other visions of the Apocalypse, seen in heaven, or descending from heaven. This glorified

THE PRESENCE IN THE MIDST

Christ appears walking in the midst[1] of seven golden lamp-stands, which are presently interpreted to mean seven churches of the Province of Asia. He is arrayed in garments which are sacerdotal, but in part also regal, the long robe of official dignity, girt with a golden girdle. It is the Priest-King, visiting the churches, making a personal examination of them all, attending to their several needs. He holds[2] in the hollow of His hand their angels—perhaps guardian angels, perhaps spirits representing the special genius, temperament, destiny of each; they are all at His disposal and in His keeping. He is in the midst, not a stationary Figure, but moving to and fro; as the Adversary *walketh*[3] *about, seeking whom he may devour*, so the great Christ, seeking whom He may save. But as He goes hither and thither, He marks what is passing in each community; the Eye of flame detects whatever is wanting or amiss, the sharp, two-edged Sword falls heavily on all insincerity, indolence, impurity—on every error whether of doctrine or of life. The differentiation of the churches that follows[4] is marked by an extraordinary minuteness which reveals intimate knowledge. It may be said that this is due to the Seer's personal acquaintance with the Christian

---

[1] Apoc. i. 13; cf. ii. 2 ὁ περιπατῶν ἐν μέσῳ τῶν ἑπτὰ ἐκκλησιῶν.
[2] In Apoc. ii. 1 ἔχων becomes κρατῶν.
[3] 1 Pet. v. 8.   [4] Apoc. ii.-iii.

brotherhoods of Asia; but even in that case it is clearly intended to represent the vigilance of the all-seeing Christ in their midst. To every church the Lord addresses the same *I know* (οἶδα), but no two churches are painted in precisely the same colours. While the general character of each church is given in a few trenchant words, exceptions are noted with scrupulous care; three [1] are praised on the whole, but with the reservation, *I have* this or that *against thee*; two [2] are censured on the whole, but in one of them, it is remarked, there are *a few names* which are worthy to walk with Christ in white, and the other is still loved and urged to repent; if the remaining two [3] are altogether commended, the grounds of the commendation are different. Not less remarkable is the adaptation of the promises with which the messages end to the circumstances or needs of each several church, and the precision with which rewards and punishments are meted out.[4] The more closely the seven words of the Spirit of Christ to the churches are studied, the more will the reader appreciate the fulness of knowledge and perfect balance of judgement which, even from the literary or historical point of view,

---

[1] Ephesus, Pergamum, Thyatira.   [2] Sardis, Laodicea.

[3] Smyrna, Philadelphia.

[4] For the details, the student is referred to Sir W. M. Ramsay's *Letters to the Seven Churches*, or to the writer's commentary on the Apocalypse.

place these little documents among the most fascinating remains of antiquity.

3. The last words of S. Matthew's Gospel, already quoted, justify the Church in expecting a presence of the Ascended Christ not only at her Eucharists and common prayers, or even in the general guidance and discipline of Christendom, but also in all efforts to fulfil her mission to the world. It is indeed in connexion with this oecumenical mission that the larger promise of His presence is given. *Go ye ... make disciples of all the nations ... and lo, I am with you alway, even unto the end of the world*[1]—even till the present order is consummated by My return. The missionaries of the Gospel never go forth alone; where they go, the Presence goes also. If they can but realize the fact, the Person who has ascended to heaven and sits on the right hand of God, exercising all authority in heaven and on earth, is Himself (ἐγώ) with the Church or her solitary representative in the most distant or hostile of heathen lands. The Lord, it will be observed, does not here limit His promise to an assembly of Christians, however small; it is also for individual Christians who are charged by His Church with the carrying out of her work. One of the new Oxyrhynchus sayings seems to express this in so many words: *wherever there are two, they are not without*

[1] Matt. xxviii. 19 f.

God; and if anywhere there is but one alone, I am with him;[1] and whatever may be thought of the genuineness of these sayings, we have the experience of S. John in Patmos to confirm the fact; not even two or three were gathered in Christ's Name when the Lord revealed Himself to the Seer of the Apocalypse. Nor can it be said that such an experience was limited to the first age. The modern missionary neither hears the voice, nor sees the majestic Form; but the Lord's *I am with you* holds good as long as the world lasts for all who give their lives to the carrying out of His great commission.[2]

Yet while the individual worker may assuredly claim the promise in his solitude, it belongs properly to the Church, and to the individual only as he represents the Body. Our Lord Himself was careful to send out His disciples by two and two;[3] so that there might never be wanting the *minimum* of an ecclesia; nor can the sending of a solitary worker into the heart of a non-Christian people be approved under any ordinary conditions. It is to the Body of Christ that the Head pledges His

---

[1] Such, at least, is a possible restoration of *Log.* 5; and in Lock and Sanday, *Two Lectures*, p. 229. The words are: ὅπου ἐὰν ὦσιν β̄, οὐκ εἰσὶν ἄθεοι, καὶ εἴ που εἷς ἐστὶν μόνος ἐγὼ εἰμὶ μετ' αὐτοῦ.

[2] The presence of the Spirit of Christ in the heart of the individual believer is another matter.

[3] Mc. vi. 7, Lc. x. 1.

presence. The Presence in the midst belongs to her in her corporate capacity, and is experienced in all her corporate activities. Whether the Church is engaged in worship or in work, the Lord Christ is with her, not only as the Eternal Word, who, being one with the Father, shares the Divine attributes, but as the glorified Son of Man. No thought can fathom this mystery, and no words can express it. But it is a fact of Christian experience, which is realized just in proportion as Christian men and women, continuing stedfastly in the unity of the Body of Christ, take their part in its sacramental life and common work. To such the Ascended Christ is not an absent but a present Lord; 'they speak as those who know that their Lord hears';[1] they work as conscious that He works with them; they worship, as though they saw Him in the midst; they live, as though He lived in them; they die, believing that He is at hand to receive their spirits. So to generation after generation the promise fulfils itself in the life of the Church, and so will it fulfil itself until *all the days* of *this age* are past, and another world opens on the perfected Body of Christ, in which the Presence of its Head will be revealed not to faith only but to sight, under the new conditions of the risen life.

[1] Tertullian, *apol.* 39: 'ita fabulantur ut qui sciant dominum audire.' 'Mc.' xvi. 20 τοῦ Κυρίου συνεργοῦντος.

IX.

THE COMING ONE.

THE Ascended Christ is present in our midst, but He is also yet to come. He is here to-day unseen; in the future He will manifest Himself by a new revelation of His glory which the Church knows as the Parousia, the Return, or the Second Advent.

1. In the New Testament the title *He that cometh* or *He that should come* (ὁ ἐρχόμενος) refers in almost every instance to the Coming in the flesh.[1] Of that first Coming our Lord Himself while on earth seems constantly to have spoken in the aorist or perfect tense: *I came*, or *I am come*.[2] But He spoke also of Comings which were future: *I come again.... I come to you.... I go away and I come to you.*[3] It would be precarious to restrict these sayings to a single future Coming; the second, at least, seems clearly to refer to the Coming of the Spirit, and the

[1] Mt. xi. 3 (Lc. vii. 20), John iii. 31, xi. 27, xii. 13. There are partial exceptions in Lc. xiii. 35, Heb. x. 37.
[2] *E.g.* Mc. ii. 17 (ἦλθον), Lc. xix. 10; Jo. xvi. 28 (ἐλήλυθα).
[3] Jo. xiv. 3, 18, 28.

THE COMING ONE

first, as we have seen, may find, at least, one fulfilment at death. But there are passages in the Gospels, and those not a few, where the Lord's words are not exhausted by any Coming of which the world has had experience. These belong with hardly an exception to the Synoptic teaching, and they shew that the Synoptic Christ expected a further coming which is yet future. *The Son of Man shall come in the glory of his Father with his angels. They shall see the Son of Man coming on the clouds of heaven with power and great glory.... Ye shall see the Son of Man sitting at the right hand of power, and coming on* (or, *with*) *the clouds of heaven.*[1] This future Coming presupposes the Ascension and glorification of the Lord's humanity, for He is seen seated as the Son of Man on the Father's Throne, and coming on the clouds attended by an angelic bodyguard. It is not necessary for our present purpose to consider whether our Lord regarded this future coming as imminent, or whether He looked for a literal fulfilment of the symbolism which He was content to adopt from the Book of Daniel or some other apocalyptic source. It is enough to say that no reasonable student of the Gospels can either doubt that the words in question are substantially those of Christ, or hold that they

[1] Mt. xvi. 27 (cf. Mc. viii. 38), xxiv. 30 (Mc. xiii. 26), xxvi. 64 (Mc. xiv. 62).

were fulfilled either by the Coming of the Spirit or the destruction of Jerusalem, or by any other event which has hitherto taken place. The Coming which they describe is clearly of another character: one which would challenge the attention of the world, and be of crucial importance to the whole human race.

And what the Master announced, the Apostolic Church as certainly expected. Christ had come both in the flesh and in the Spirit, but they looked for yet another Coming which was to bring the Lord back to them in the full glory of His exalted manhood. Even as they gazed up after Him into heaven, they heard angelic voices declare, *This Jesus... shall so come in like manner as ye beheld him going into heaven.*[1] There must some day be a reversal of the Ascension; He who went to the Father shall come back to His Church, and come as He went. This belief passed at once into the preaching of the Church, and became a prominent feature in the primitive Gospel. *Repent*, the first preachers urged, *...that so there may come seasons of refreshing from the presence of the Lord, and that he may send the Christ who hath been appointed for you, even Jesus: whom the heaven must receive until the times of restoration of all things.*[2] How largely this hope of another and more glorious Advent entered into S. Paul's early

[1] Acts i. 11.   [2] Acts iii. 19 ff.

THE COMING ONE 131

teaching of the Gentile churches appears from the Epistles to the Thessalonians, his first extant letters. *Ye turned,* he writes to the Thessalonians, *unto God from idols, to serve a living and true God, and to wait for his Son from heaven, whom he raised from the dead, even Jesus, which delivereth us from the wrath to come.*[1] It is clear that the expectation of the coming Saviour filled a foremost place in the primitive Christianity of the Pauline character. Already a Greek term had been found for the expected Advent: four times in this one Epistle[2] it is spoken of as the *Parousia*, a word which, like the Latin *adventus*, is used in nearly contemporary documents for the state-visit of the Emperor to a province or city in his dominions.[3] S. Paul's letter must have added greatly to the keenness of the interest with which the Thessalonian Christians regarded the Advent, for it contains an apocalyptic description of the coming event which goes beyond the words of Christ recorded in the Gospels: *the Lord himself shall descend from heaven with a shout of command, with the voice of the archangel and with the trump of God, and the dead*

---

[1] 1 Th. i. 9.   [2] 1 Thess. ii. 19, iii. 13, iv. 15, v. 23.

[3] See G. Milligan, *Thessalonians*, p. 145 ff.: Deissmann, *Light from the Ancient East*, E. tr. p. 372 ff. The wide use of the term in other Christian circles appears from its occurrence in James v. 7 f; 1 Jo. ii. 28; Mt. xxiv. 3, 27, 37, 39. It occurs, however, also in reference to the arrival of an ordinary person, *e.g.* Stephanas (1 Cor. xvi. 17), Titus (2 Cor. vii. 6 f), S. Paul himself (Phil. i. 26, ii. 12), so that the Imperial character of the visit must not be unduly pressed.

in Christ shall rise first; then we that are alive, that are left, shall together with them be caught up in the clouds to meet the Lord in the air; and so shall we ever be with the Lord.[1] It is scarcely surprising that the enthusiasm of his converts got the better of their reason,[2] especially since they were led to infer from the Apostle's words that the day of the Lord had already begun (ἐνέστηκεν). The second letter is occupied with the correction of this error: Christ could not come before Antichrist, and the advent (παρουσία, v. 9) of Antichrist was at present held back by the forces of law and order which were represented by the Roman Empire. Thus the Advent of the Lord and the gathering to Him of the Church was not even imminent, and all the duties of life must go forward in their ordinary course while the Church was waiting for that day. After this early experience of the excitable temperament of his Greek converts, S. Paul perhaps deliberately practised more reserve when he dealt with the doctrine of the Last Things. There are, indeed, passages which shew that he did not go back from his first convictions: the glowing description in 1 Corinthians of the effect to be produced on the saints by the Parousia: *we shall all be changed, in a moment, in the twinkling of an eye, at the last trump; for the trumpet shall sound, and the dead shall be raised incorruptible, and we*

---

[1] 1 Thess. iv. 16 f.   [2] 2 Thess. ii. 2 σαλευθῆναι ὑμᾶς ἀπὸ τοῦ νοός.

—the living—*shall be changed*;[1] and the similar, but briefer, passage in Philippians: *our citizenship is in heaven, from whence also we wait for a Saviour, the Lord Jesus Christ, who shall fashion anew the body of our humiliation, that it may be conformed to the body of his glory.*[2] But the references to the Coming in S. Paul's later letters are usually free from apocalyptic detail; and he is content to speak in a general way of the revelation (ἀποκάλυψις) of Christ, or of His manifestation or epiphany (ἐπιφάνεια).[3] Yet if the symbolism disappears, the hope remains, and the theological insight becomes even more penetrating. Everywhere in S. Paul's Epistles, early or late, the note of the future Coming is heard. It is the Advent and not death which is the recognized *terminus* of life; *until the Lord come, till he come,*[4] marks the limit of the present provisional order; *Maran atha,* 'our Lord cometh'[5] (or, perhaps, 'come!') is the great Christian watchword which, though expressed in Aramaic—derived, it may be, from the mother church of Palestine—was intelligible to a church so thoroughly

---

[1] 1 Cor. xv. 51 f. [2] Phil. iii. 20 f.

[3] 1 Cor. i. 7 f., Phil. ii. 16, Col. iii. 1, 1 Tim. vi. 14, 2 Tim. iv. 1, 8, Tit. ii. 13. On ἐπιφάνεια see G. Milligan on Thessalonians, p. 148 f.; the history of the word is even more instructive than that of παρουσία. In 2 Thess. ii. 8 the two words are combined (ἐπιφ. τῆς παρουσίας αὐτοῦ).

[4] 1 Cor. iv. 5, xi. 26.

[5] 1 Cor. xvi. 22; cf. *Didache* 10, where it occurs, followed by ἀμήν, as an Eucharistic formula.

Greek as that of Corinth. In the two great Christological Epistles to the Ephesians and the Colossians there is but little direct mention of the Advent; yet the great hope sparkles in every reference to the future inheritance of the Church;[1] while in the Pastoral Epistles, which, if they are S. Paul's, must belong to his last years, the veteran Apostle finds it the chief support of his failing strength: *I have fought the good fight .... henceforth there is laid up for me the crown of righteousness, which the Lord, the righteous judge, shall give to me at that day; and not only to me, but also to all them that have loved his appearing.*[2] All who shared the Apostle's faith must share, he was assured, his longing for the Advent, *looking for the blessed hope and appearing of the glory of our great God and Saviour Jesus Christ.*[3]

Nor is this a Pauline doctrine only. The author of Hebrews[4] works it into his teaching on the Highpriesthood of Christ; our High Priest, who is now within the veil, shall *appear a second time* (ἐκ δευτέρου) to the members of His Church who wait for Him in the outer court,[5] and for these His Return shall be *unto salvation.* S. Peter sees in the Coming an unveiling of the glory which belongs to the person of Jesus Christ, but hitherto has been hidden from

---

[1] See *e.g.* Eph. i. 10, 14, 18, ii. 7, iii. 21, iv. 13, v. 27; Col. i. 12, iii. 4.

[2] 2 Tim. iv. 7 f.   [3] Titus ii. 13.   [4] Heb. ix. 28.   [5] Cf. Lev. xvi. 24.

THE COMING ONE

the sight of the world by the intervening veil of the flesh.[1] S. John, towards the end of the century, falls back on the old word *Parousia* which had been the favourite of S. Paul: with him the Advent is the coming of the Lord to visit again the scenes of His earthly life, and the servants who are charged to do His work in the world.[2] The Apocalypse rings with the voice of Christ Himself testifying, *I come quickly,* and its last word is the response of the Bride, *Amen, come, Lord Jesus.*[3] Even the Epistle of James, with its *minimum* of Christian doctrine, recognizes *the coming of the Lord.*[4]

2. The New Testament, then, with one consent, in Gospels, Acts, Epistles, Apocalypse, proclaims a future Return of the Ascended Lord. There is no dissentient voice; there is scarcely one which is wholly silent on the subject. As surely as the Lord ascended, He will come again. The Creeds are nowhere on surer ground than when to *ascendit in caelos* they add, *Unde venturus est*—' from thence He shall come.' Nevertheless, to many minds this article presents insuperable difficulties. They think of it as involving a literal fulfilment of the apocalyptic symbolism of the Second Coming which the New Testament inherits from the Book of Daniel. They imagine the Ascension literally reversed, and

[1] 1 Pet. i. 7, 13, iv. 13. [2] 1 Jo. ii. 28.
[3] Apoc. iii. 11, xxii. 12, 20. [4] James v. 7.

the intellectual difficulties of the scene vastly increased. 'He shall come' means, they suppose, that He shall visibly descend in a chariot of clouds, accompanied by visible hosts of superhuman beings. These conceptions can of course be justified by an appeal to the letter of Scripture, but so can also the vision of the Great White Throne and the Open Books. Difficulties of this kind would be lessened if it were remembered that the Coming of the Lord, according to the New Testament, synchronizes with the change which is to convert flesh and blood into a spiritual and incorruptible body. It is clear from this consideration, that the final Epiphany, will not be such as to appeal to our present organs of sense; the descriptions which represent it as such cannot therefore be interpreted literally. It may indeed be that the change which will pass over us will itself be the unveiling or epiphany or advent of the hidden Christ. He is hidden from us now through the grossness of our *body of humiliation*; at the moment when this is *conformed to the body of his glory*[1] the veil will be taken away, and the eternal opened up to sight. In any case, the essential truth conveyed by the symbolical descriptions of the Advent is that a day is coming when the glory of Jesus Christ shall be revealed to all mankind. *Ye shall see the Son of Man sitting at the right hand of Power, and*

[1] Phil. iii. 20 f.

THE COMING ONE 137

coming with the clouds of heaven.[1] *Every eye shall see him, and they which pierced him.*[2] The vision of the Coming Christ, it is clear, is not to be restricted to the saints; His bitterest enemies shall share it.

It must be confessed that it is hard to understand by what means the exalted Christ can be revealed to the non-Christian world. How shall Caiaphas and the Sanhedrin, Herod and Pontius Pilate, Nero and Domitian be made to see the Son of Man in the glory of the Father? It may be that in that supreme moment of human history, when all the dead, great and small, stand before God, the Spirit of Christ will so convict the whole world of sin, of righteousness, and of judgement, that all opposition will be disarmed and all incapacity overcome. But in whatever way, the revelation, it appears, is to be made to all: a revelation which, to those who do not love the Lord, must be one of unspeakable awe, bringing confusion of face and grief of heart. *All the tribes of the earth shall mourn over him,*[3] whether with *the sorrow of the world* that *worketh death*, or *after a Godly sort*, working in the end *repentance unto salvation*[4]—if it is not, indeed, too late for any true turning to Him whom they pierced.

To the Church the final Advent will not be a

[1] Mc. xiv. 62. [2] Apoc. i. 7.
[3] Apoc. i. 7. [4] 2 Cor. vii. 9 f.

momentary flash of blinding light, revealing the glory of the Lord and then dying out into the blackness of despair, but the lasting consummation of her faith and hope and labour of love. It will be more than even this. The Church is not only to see the glory of the Ascended Christ, but to share it. He and His are to be *glorified together*.[1] The *revealing of the sons of God*, for which the whole creation waits, will accompany the revelation of the Only Begotten Son. He comes *to be glorified in his saints*;[2] their spiritual bodies will *bear the image of the Heavenly*,[3] being *conformed to the body of his glory*,[4] and shining forth *as the sun in the Kingdom of their Father*.[5] The glorification of Christ and the conglorification of the Saints are related as cause and effect: *if he shall be manifested, we shall be like him, for we shall see him even as he is*.[6] Yet, so far as we can judge, the two processes will, in fact, be simultaneous. As the whole stupendous scene impressed itself on the imagination of S. Paul, *the dead in Christ*, who are already in some sense with the Lord, *will God bring with him*; while the living, changed *as in a moment*, shall *together with them be caught up in the clouds, to meet the Lord in the air*.[7] His coming will be theirs; they will come with Him.

---

[1] Rom. viii. 17 ff. (ἵνα συνδοξασθῶμεν).
[2] 2 Th. i. 10.   [3] 1 Cor. xv. 44 ff.   [4] Phil. iii. 20.
[5] Mt. xiii. 43.   [6] 1 Jo. iii. 2.   [7] 1 Th. iv. 14 ff.

THE COMING ONE

The great future belongs to Jesus Christ and to His Church. This is the ultimate meaning of New Testament apocalyptic. Our Lord is the Coming One. When or how He shall come we know not; generations may have to run their course first, and in the end the Advent may be far other than we anticipate. But of one thing we are assured by our Christian faith: beyond the furthest limits of human history there is an age of fuller knowledge, larger power, more splendid achievements, a more perfect life, than the existing order can attain to. No progress of scientific discovery, no changes of social conditions, no system of education or politics or ethical principles, can abolish Pain or Death or Sin; only the faith of Christ can promise that *Death shall be no more, neither shall there be mourning nor crying nor pain any more; the first things are passed away . . . and there shall in no wise enter . . . anything unclean.*[1] This painless, deathless, sinless future comes with the Ascended Christ; He has already entered it, and He will bring it with Him to the world. Who that has this hope in Him will not take up the call of the Spirit and the Bride, and say *Come?*[2] *Amen: come, Lord Jesus.*

[1] Apoc. xxi. 4, 27.   [2] Apoc. xxii. 17, 20.

X.

THE JUDGE.

THE Creeds of Christendom connect the coming of the Lord with the judgement of mankind. He comes 'to judge the quick and the dead,'[1] that is, all the generations of the human race, from the first to that which shall be alive at the time of His coming. Thus the faith of the Church (*a*) invests the Ascended Christ with the office of Judge, and (*b*) connects His fulfilment of this office with the Parousia.

1. In His Galilean teaching our Lord appears to have repeatedly represented Himself as the supreme arbiter of the destinies of all members of His Church. His sayings on this subject belong largely to the eschatological parables of S. Matthew and S. Luke, and are clothed in pictorial language borrowed from the life of the people. Jesus is the husbandman who, *in the time of harvest ... will say to the reapers, Gather up first the tares, and bind them in bundles to*

---

[1] So the Apostles' Creed: 'unde venturus est iudicare vivos et mortuos.' The 'Nicene' Creed has: πάλιν ἐρχόμενον μετὰ δόξης κρῖναι ζῶντας καὶ νεκρούς.

THE JUDGE

burn them: but gather the wheat into my barn.[1] Or, He is the bridegroom who refuses to open the door to the belated virgins; or the master who takes the talent from the slothful servant and gives it to the good and faithful.[2] Once, according to S. Matthew, Jesus said plainly, *The Son of Man shall come in the glory of his Father with his angels, and then shall he render unto every man according to his deeds*;[3] and once the judgement is expressly extended to the whole world: *then shall he sit on the throne of his glory: and before him shall be gathered all the nations.*[4]

In the fourth Gospel this conception of Christ as the Judge of men is developed and interpreted. The *locus classicus* upon the subject is the great discourse which our Lord bases on the text, *My Father worketh even until now, and I work*:[5] *What things soever* the Father *doeth*, He continues, *these the Son also doeth in like manner.* Some things there are which the Father has given wholly into the hands of the Son: *neither doth the Father judge any man, but he hath given all judgement unto the Son.... He gave him authority to execute judgement, because he is son of man* (ὅτι υἱὸς ἀνθρώπου ἐστίν). It is, then,

---

[1] Mt. xiii. 30; cf. v. 41.   [2] Mt. xxv. 11 f., 28.

[3] Mt. xvi. 27. S. Mark (viii. 38) has this saying in a simpler and perhaps earlier form.

[4] Mt. xxv. 31.   [5] Jo. v. 17 ff.

the Son as incarnate who is the appointed Judge; because, being Son of God, He is also man. His manhood fits Him to undertake the office of Judge of mankind, as His unique relation to the Father makes it possible for Him to do so.

Even during His earthly life the judicial aspect of our Lord's mission comes into light. It was not, indeed, to execute judgement that He came in the flesh. *God sent not the Son into the world to judge the world, but that the world should be saved through him. I judge no man*, the Lord declares; *I came not to judge the world, but to save the world.* Yet elsewhere He says: *for judgement* (εἰς κρίμα) *came I into the world.*[1] S. John, who records these apparently contradictory sayings, explains how a coming which was not for the purpose of judging men might nevertheless be *unto judgement; this*, he writes, *is the judgement, that the Light is come into the world, and men loved the darkness rather than the Light; for their deeds were evil.* Judgement, as the New Testament uses the word, is separation between good and bad—the manifestation, whether by circumstances or by an authoritative sentence, of the inherent, essential incompatibility of the two. Our English term and its cognates are forensic: they speak of the court of law, with its rigid formalism, its externality, its occasional travesties of justice.

[1] Jo. iii. 17, viii. 15, ix. 39, xii. 47.

THE JUDGE

But the series of Greek words which we translate by 'judge' and 'judgement' (κρίνειν, κριτής, κρίσις, κρίμα) strikes another note; it tells of the spiritual distinctions which exist between man and man, and must ultimately be brought to light: it has regard to the moral grounds on which all true judgement rests.

During the Ministry our Lord Himself passed no judgement, conscious though He was that if He judged, His judgement would be true.[1] Yet His presence among the Jewish people did, in fact, bring to light the true character of every man who heard His call; and the attitude of each individual towards the Christ shewed what manner of man he was, and determined his position in the spiritual world. All who were brought into contact with Jesus thus passed judgement on themselves, for none who encountered the Light of the world could remain neutral; *he that is not with me is against me*[2] is a canon which is absolutely true in principle, though its application may be precarious in the hands of those who are no judges of the secrets of the heart. In the sight of God he who shuns the Light is self-condemned (ἤδη κέκριται): he has pronounced sentence on himself by his refusal of the Truth. This process was not limited to the days of our Lord's visible presence; the Gospel and the Church still carry it forward in the world. The dividing line between

---
[1] Jo. viii. 16. [2] Mt. xii. 30.

man and man is drawn in the sight of God by the attitude which each soul that hears the call of the Gospel in the Church assumes towards Jesus Christ. This of course is not in all cases equivalent to its attitude towards the Church or towards orthodox belief; invincible prejudice or ignorance may lead a man to oppose both, while his heart is on the side of Christ. But the alternative to essential sympathy with Christ is aversion to Him, and the presence of one or other of these attitudes determines the spiritual position of the individual in the sight of God. The picture drawn by S. John[1] of our Lord on the Cross—*on either side one, and Jesus in the midst*—typifies the general result of the preaching of the Cross, and anticipates the final issue.: *before him shall be gathered all nations, and he shall separate them one from another, as the shepherd separateth the sheep from the goats: and he shall set the sheep on his right hand, but the goats on the left.*[2] The Person of Christ divides men now, and will divide them in the end; here and hereafter He is the Judge.

2. There may have been, and may be in time to come, many epochs in the history of individuals, of nations, and of the world, which are in a special sense 'days of judgement';[3] critical seasons, which

---

[1] Jo. xix. 18.   [2] Mt. xxv. 31 ff.
[3] For [ἡ] ἡμέρα [τῆς] κρίσεως, see Mt. x. 15, xi. 22, 24, xii. 36; 2 Pet. ii. 9, iii. 7; 1 Jo. iv. 17. The phrase occurs also in Enoch xxii. 4, Ps. Sol. xv. 12.

THE JUDGE

manifest character, and perhaps bring it to its maturity. But all such days culminate in the 'great day' or 'last day,'[1] the 'day of the Lord' or 'of Christ,' the *day of wrath and revelation of the righteous judgement of God*.[2] In a startling phrase S. Paul once contrasts 'man's day' (ἀνθρωπίνη ἡμέρα) with the Lord's—the preliminary assize in which men sit in judgement upon the conduct or motives of their fellows, with the final issues of life as they will be made apparent by the coming of Jesus Christ. Judged by false brethren at Corinth, he reserves himself for the hearing of the Supreme Arbiter who is ever at hand: *it is a very small thing that I should be judged* (ἀνακριθῶ) *of you or by man's day* (ὑπ' ἀνθρωπίνης ἡμέρας) *... he that judgeth me is the Lord. Wherefore judge nothing before the time, until the Lord come*.[3]

The Apostolic age, it cannot be doubted, looked for a particular day or epoch when all the results of the present life must be passed under examination, and judgement be pronounced upon them by the Ascended Christ.[4] It is also clear that this period of scrutiny, this 'summing up of the aeon,'[5] as it is

---

[1] Jude 6 εἰς κρίσιν μεγάλης ἡμέρας. Jo. vi. 39 f., 44, 54 [ἐν] τῇ ἐσχάτῃ ἡμέρᾳ.

[2] Rom. ii. 5.   [3] 1 Cor. iv. 3 ff.

[4] 1 Cor. i. 8, v. 5; Phil. i. 6, 10; ii. 16; 1 Th. v. 2; 2 Th. ii. 2.

[5] Mt. xiii. 39 f., 49; xxiv. 3, xxviii. 20 [ἡ] συντέλεια τοῦ αἰῶνος: Heb. ix. 26 has [ἡ] συντέλεια τῶν αἰώνων.

called in the first Gospel, was connected by the first age with the manifestation of the glorified Son of Man at the Parousia. Whatever the event or course of events might be which would fulfil the promise of the Lord's coming, it would also bring about the final Judgement. We may go far wrong in our interpretation of the details; as to the main point there is no possibility of error.

It may serve as a warning against the tendency to press apocalyptic details, if we reflect upon the great variety of the symbolism employed by our Lord when He speaks of His own coming. It is a stormy day in the winter season, when the rains descend and the floods come and the winds blow, and the world, like one of the wadys of Palestine, is turned into a raging, howling waste of waters, in which no house without foundation can live.[1] It is the time of harvest, and the wheat is being gathered into sheaves for garnering; but first the weeds are bound in bundles for the fire.[2] It is a night of festivity; crowds are pouring in to the brilliantly lighted banqueting hall; at the last moment one of the invited guests is cast out into the darkness of the night.[3] It is a day on which the Master of a great house has suddenly returned from his travels; the major domo has been surprised in the midst of his cups, and he is cut asunder with one blow of his

---

[1] Mt. vii. 24 ff.   [2] Mt. xiii. 30, 42.   [3] Mt. xxii. 11 ff.

THE JUDGE 147

lord's great sword.¹ It is as when Noah's flood burst on a thoughtless, merry-making age, or the rain of fire and brimstone descended on the cities of the plain.² These pictures, it is evident, call up incompatible scenes; though each in its own way may reflect some feature in the final catastrophe, not one of them can be taken to represent it except in the way of suggestion.

The same must be said of the apocalyptic language, chiefly borrowed from the Old Testament, in which more direct descriptions of the Judgement are clothed : so far as they present to the mind physical phenomena, they can be but efforts to assist it in conceiving of spiritual processes which are beyond present experience and for that reason cannot find direct expression in human words.

There are, however, certain ideas which are common to all or to most of these representations, whether parabolic or apocalyptic, and may therefore be safely regarded as of the essence of our Lord's revelation in reference to the future Judgement. It is certain, for example, that He claims for Himself as the Son of Man the office of Supreme Judge. He comes in the glory of the Father, as the Father's plenipotentiary; it is the glorified Christ and not the invisible God who is to conduct the scrutiny and pass the sentence; here, as in all dealings of

¹ Lc. xii. 43 ff.   ² Lc. xvii. 26 ff.

God with man, He is Mediator between God and man. This, it will be observed, is precisely the teaching of the fourth Gospel, where it is stated in direct words: the Son will judge *because he is son of man*. Again, the Synoptists, equally with S. John, represent the Judgement as essentially a process of division, which will strictly follow the facts of life, so that the work of the Judge is merely to reveal the true character of each individual, and thereby to assign to him his place in the new spiritual order which begins with His appearing. Once more, the Synoptic parables and apocalyptic sayings shew us Christendom falling, under the light of the Coming, into two vast multitudes, in one or other of which each individual must find his own place, and within which there will therefore be, as it seems, as many gradations as there are types of character or varieties of moral and spiritual condition. The popular view which recognizes no distinctions in future rewards or punishments is clearly at variance with our Lord's Synoptic teaching.[1] As to the finality of the award, we go perhaps beyond His words if we assert that it is final in such a sense as to fix character and destiny irrevocably. The Lord's words refer to the new age which His Return inaugurates: of those far distant aeons which S. Paul sees coming up one behind the other like

---

[1] See, *e.g.* Lc. xii. 47 f., xix. 17.

THE JUDGE

great ocean waves reaching into the immeasurable distance of the future,[1] we can say nothing. Yet, on the other hand, it is a significant fact that the whole system of Christ's mediation seems to come to an end with the Parousia, nor is there any intimation that God has in store fresh opportunities of repentance and grace for those who have refused the Light while it was with them. It is best to confess our ignorance where Scripture fails us, and to limit ourselves to the tremendous certainty that the judgement of Christ will place each man in that precise relation to the next age of which his conduct in this life has made him capable.

So much may be learnt from the teaching of our Lord Himself as it is reported in the Gospels. The Apostolic age inherited this teaching and handed it on. 'Eternal judgement' was one of *the first principles of Christ*[2] which the early missionaries of the Church delivered to their converts, and it took its place once for all in the primitive creed of Christendom. To the heathen it was preached as a fundamental and most necessary truth; it will be remembered how S. Paul insisted upon it at Athens, and before Felix.[3] His Epistles dwell more often on the hope set before the Church than upon the judgement of the world; but occasional references to the Judgement shew that

---

[1] Eph. ii. 7 ἐν τοῖς αἰῶσιν τοῖς ἐπερχομένοις.   [2] Heb. vi. 1 ff.
[3] Acts xvii. 30 f., xxiv. 25.

believers themselves need to find a place for it in their thoughts of the Lord's future coming. *He that judgeth me is the Lord.*[1] *We must all be made manifest before the judgement seat of Christ, that each one may receive the things done in the body, according to what he hath done, whether it be good or bad.*[2] *God shall judge the secrets of men, according to my gospel, by Jesus Christ.*[3] *Christ Jesus ... shall judge the quick and the dead ... the righteous judge shall give to me* the crown of righteousness *at that day.*[4] As he writes these passages two scenes from the experience of his own life in Gentile cities pass before the Apostle's eyes. He sees the proconsul seated on his tribunal ($\beta\hat{\eta}\mu a$), administering the law with the impartial justice that was still characteristic of Roman judges;[5] and the umpire of the races at the stadium ($\beta\rho a\beta\epsilon\acute{u}s$) holding out a wreath of pine to the successful runner.[6] Quite different from both conceptions, but perhaps even more impressive, is the great Judgement scene in the Apocalypse: *I saw a great white throne, and him that sat upon it, from whose face the earth and the heaven fled away; and there was found no place for them. And I saw the dead, the great and the small, standing before the throne; and books were opened: and another book*

---

[1] 1 Cor. iv. 3 f.
[2] 2 Cor. v. 10.
[3] Rom. ii. 16.
[4] 2 Tim. iv. 1, 7.
[5] Cf. Acts xviii. 12 ff.
[6] 1 Cor. ix. 24, Col. ii. 18.

THE JUDGE

was opened, which is the Book of Life: and the dead were judged out of the things which were written in the books, according to their works.[1] Here there is little which is peculiarly Christian, and even the mediation of Christ is not hinted at. The imagery is almost wholly taken from the Old Testament—the opened books are from Daniel,[2] and the idea of the Book of Life is already found in Exodus; both were familiar to the Jewish apocalyptic writers. It is the Eternal Father who sits on the throne, and not, as in Christian pictures of the Judgement, the Incarnate Son.[3] There is no mention of the living, or of the change which will pass over them at the coming of the Lord; His coming does not enter into the vision. But if in this one passage the Seer reiterates ideas about the Judgement which Jews shared with Christians, in other places he gives full expression to those which are purely Christian. The Reaper of the Harvest of the Earth who comes seated on a white cloud is *one like unto a son of man*. The Holy City of the Saints is seen *coming down out of heaven from God, made ready as a bride adorned for her husband: the lamp*

---

[1] Apoc. xx. 11 ff.

[2] Dan. vii. 10, Exod. xxxii. 32. Cf. Enoch xlvii. 3, xc. 20; *Apoc. Baruch* xxiv. 1.

[3] Yet even S. Paul speaks of the βῆμα τοῦ θεοῦ (Rom. xiv. 10), as well as τοῦ χριστοῦ (2 Cor. v. 10). God will judge in and by Christ.

thereof is the Lamb, and its inhabitants are *they which are written in the Lamb's Book of Life.* Lastly, Christ is heard to say, in words which remind us of the first Gospel, *Behold, I come quickly; and my reward is with me, to render to each man according as his work is.*[1]

Thus the whole of the New Testament witnesses with one voice, although with much variety of metaphor, to the coming of a Day of Judgement, which is coincident with the coming of the Lord. It may be that all the descriptions of the Great Day are to be interpreted as symbolical pictures which await their true interpretation when the day arrives; it may be that the Day itself is an epoch in human history rather than a space of time to be measured by hours. But such considerations do not touch the central truth, which remains as S. Paul stated it when he stood in the midst of the Areopagus, facing the frivolous Athenians of his time. *God... hath appointed a day in the which he will judge the world in righteousness by the Man whom he hath ordained; whereof he hath given assurance unto all men, in that he hath raised him from the dead.*[2] The Resurrection and Ascension point with awful certainty to the coming Judgement of the world.

[1] Apoc. xiv. 14 ff., xxi. 2, 23, 27, xxii. 12; cf. Matt. xvi. 27.
[2] Acts xvii. 30 f.

'We believe that thou shalt come to be our Judge. We therefore pray thee, help thy servants, whom thou hast redeemed with thy precious blood. Make them to be numbered with thy Saints in glory everlasting. O Lord, save thy people, and bless thine heritage; govern them, and lift them up for ever.'

POSTSCRIPT.

It may be asked, To what purpose is such a study of the work of the Ascended Christ? Can any subject which is so transcendent that it cannot be expressed in the terms of human experience without calling in the aid of symbolism, be of practical value to our modern life? May it not safely be left to mystical theologians, while Christians in general devote themselves to problems which lie nearer to the heart of religion and morality?

To many it may not seem sufficient to answer that in the judgement of the leaders of the Apostolic age the life of Christ in heaven must have had a supreme value, seeing that it forms almost the chief subject of their teaching. Circumstances have changed, it will be said, and the present age needs to have its attention directed to matters of more immediate interest, such as the intellectual and social problems which beset us to-day, and clamour for a speedy solution.

In view of this objection it may be worth while to count up a few of the religious ends which are to be gained in these days by studying the life and functions of the Exalted Christ.

1. The Ascension and Ascended Life bear witness against the materialistic spirit which threatens in some quarters to overpower those higher interests that have their seat in the region of the spiritual and eternal. They are as a *Sursum corda*—'lift up your hearts'—which comes down from the High Priest of the Church who stands at the heavenly altar, and draws forth from the kneeling Church the answer *Habemus ad Dominum*—'we lift them up unto the Lord.' Faith in the Ascended Christ was S. Paul's remedy for the sensuality which he encountered in the Greek cities of Asia Minor: *seek the things that are above, where Christ is, seated on the right hand of God. Set your mind on the things that are above, not on the things that are upon the earth; for your life is hid with Christ in God; mortify therefore your members which are upon the earth.* How strong a motive this appeal supplied is evident from the history of the primitive Church. The grosser vices of paganism have less attraction for our age, but the downward pressure of external things remains; at a time when life is being reduced to a complex machinery for the production of wealth, there is ample room for a doctrine which points men persistently to an order

of realities which are at once present and eternal, a world which already surrounds us and waits only for the coming of the Lord to be manifested in overwhelming power.

2. The faith of the Ascended Life is not less necessary as a safeguard against minimizing estimates of the Person and Work of Jesus Christ. To judge of His position in the universe by the records of His earthly life alone is to take into account but one of the two great factors on which the Church has based her creed, and the one which is the less decisive. The Christ of the New Testament is a person who not only lived and died on the earth, but who rose again, and in His risen humanity ascended to heaven, and from that day to the present hour lives and reigns there. If we choose to limit ourselves to the Jesus of history, and proceed to tear away from the records of His life the supernatural element which was woven into the texture of the primitive gospel, it is doubtless within our power to maintain a purely humanitarian view of the Person of our Lord; or, if we prefer it, to decline to examine the question of His relation to God, as one that does not call for an answer. But no such position is possible for those who frankly accept the teaching of the New Testament as a whole. The glorified Christ of the Epistles and Apocalypse is not 'mere man.' As we gaze

POSTSCRIPT

at the heavenly vision, we see that, if it represents a reality, S. Paul must have been right when he said that Jesus pre-existed *in the form of God*, and S. John, when he identified Him with the Word who *was with God and was God*. And as it is with the Person, so it is also with the Work of Christ; the Ascension has lifted it to a plane immeasurably higher than that of the earthly life, high as that stands above the lives of other men, and has extended it to far wider fields of energy. The Gospels reveal our Lord as Teacher, Healer, Master, *Pastor pastorum*; and in all these relations, He is incomparable. Again, they shew Him tempted, suffering, dying, and victorious over temptation, pain, and death; and these aspects of the Christ-life are beyond price. But how much remains of His work, at which the Gospels hardly hint? His mediation and intercession, His high-priestly life of perpetual self-presentation, His reign, His exercise of universal authority, His certainty of complete victory; His gift of the Spirit, His Headship of the Church, His office of universal Judge :—this is the contribution which is made by the second half of the New Testament to our knowledge of Christ. When all this is left out of sight, can we wonder that men do not get beyond a humanitarian view of His Person, and an equally defective conception of His Mission? To the Christian who is content to follow the teaching of the Apostolic age there is no such alternative as 'Jesus or Christ'; the Jesus of the Gospels is the Christ of the Epistles, and he cannot even in thought dissociate the Exalted Being portrayed in the latter from the Son of Mary who was crucified; the two pictures are those of one person in two stages of His history, and both stages belong equally to the human life of the Word made flesh.

3. The New Testament doctrine of the Ascension is also necessary to a right understanding of the office and powers of the Catholic Church. The estimate which men form of the Church, and their sense of the privilege and responsibility of membership in that great Body, vary according to the vividness or the dimness of vision with which they realize the ascension of the Church's Head. It is not strange that persons who take little interest in the heavenly life of Jesus Christ, regard the Church as a merely human society, or a department of the State—a force to be respected and supported as it makes for good order and public morality, but possessing no supernatural powers or authority, and, apart from the law of the land, or the obligation of a voluntary compact, no claim upon the submission of the human mind and will. Nor is it matter for surprise that men of this type ignore the corporate life of the Church, contending that

personal religion is sufficient for their spiritual needs. Such an attitude, common as it is among modern Christians, was perhaps altogether unknown to primitive Christianity. In the first days the Christian Society bulked larger than the individual member, not that the religion of the individual life was undervalued, but that the life of the Body was felt to be something greater and more precious. The language which S. Paul uses in reference to the Church may seem at times to be extravagant: the Church, he says, is the fulness of Christ, the Body of Christ, the city of the Saints, the household of God; through the Church is made known to the heavenly powers the manifold wisdom of God; the Church is hereafter to be presented by Christ to Himself glorious, without spot or blemish; even now it is the pillar and ground of the truth. If it be asked how an association of mortal and sinful men can support these astounding claims, the answer is to be found in her intimate relation to the Ascended Christ. All His power, all His life, is hers. The Church, alone among human societies, has a Head in heaven, and thus is linked to the eternal and infinite. She has, it is true, an earthly side and an outward life, which place her in relation with the world; and allowance must be made for these in her attitude towards society and the State. So long as the State recognizes the Church, and secures to her the enjoyment of the property and dignities which she inherits from the piety of older generations, we use it gladly; but no one who believes in the Church's relation to the glorified Lord would esteem her less highly if she were despoiled and degraded, or even, as in the first days, compelled to flee into the wilderness from the face of the Dragon. She would still be the Body, the Bride of Christ; and Christ lives and reigns at the right hand of God.

4. Faith in the Ascended Christ dictates the attitude which the Church should maintain towards the world. Two mistakes have been made in reference to this matter. There have been times in the life of the Church when she has been tempted to make common cause with the world, or to meet it halfway; and times, again, when she has gone to the opposite extreme of retiring from the world altogether. Neither of these attitudes is Apostolic or primitive, for in the early days of the faith, when men lived in full view of the Ascended Life, they knew how to live in the world without being of it. There is a familiar passage in a second century Apology which puts this into words, and must be quoted here once again. 'Christians,' the writer says, 'are not distinguished from the rest of mankind either by country or speech or customs. They neither inhabit cities of their own, nor use a

different language, nor practise a manner of life which is out of the common.... But while inhabiting cities Greek or foreign, as the lot of each determines, and following the customs of the country both in regard to dress and food and life in general, they shew themselves to be possessed of a citizenship which is all their own, and the nature of it is a paradox. They dwell in their native lands, but as sojourners; they share all things as citizens and endure all things as strangers; every foreign country is their fatherland, and every fatherland a foreign country to them.... They are in the flesh, but do not live after the flesh; they pass their time on earth, but they live their lives as citizens in heaven.'[1] This is a healthier and truer type of 'other-worldliness' than that which was adopted by the ascetic ages that followed, and it rests on the conviction that, while our Master who is in heaven has given us a *status* there, and will come again to receive us to Himself, our place and work are meanwhile by His appointment on this earth, and among our fellowmen. The life of the Church has, in fact, a twofold character: it is *hid with Christ in God*, and yet and at the same time is to shine as a guiding light before men. Any age that overlooks either of these sides of the Christian life, or exaggerates one of them at the expense of the

[1] *Ep. ad Diognetum*, 5.

other, suffers spiritual loss; and it suffers because it has failed to realize the full significance of the Ascension and the Return in their relation to the present duty of the Church as representing Christ in the world.

5. To realize the work of our Lord in heaven is essential to any right appreciation of the worship of the Church. If many persons who profess to be Christians forsake the assembling of themselves together for common prayer and praise and Eucharist, it is because the vision of the High Priest who is within the veil, and yet in the midst of every assembly of His Church, has taken no real hold upon their faith. Apart from the High-priestly life in heaven, prayer is a venture, with no assurance of success; apart from the real presence of the Ascended Christ in our assemblies, common prayer has no special value. To those who take little or no account of the Ascended Life, the Sacraments may well seem to be empty ceremonies, which are to be observed as a matter of convention or at most as an act of obedience to a positive command. Such persons can see in Baptism only a symbol of spiritual regeneration, and in the Eucharist, the memorial of a dead or absent Christ. Confirmation, in like manner, is in their eyes no more than a renewal of the Baptismal promises, and Absolution a mere declaration of God's readiness to forgive the penitent. All this is changed so soon as the fruits of

POSTSCRIPT 163

the Ascension are apprehended; the Ascended Christ is seen to be present and operative in His Church, Himself by His Spirit regenerating His members in Baptism, and strengthening the young life in Confirmation; giving His own Body and Blood in Holy Communion; remitting the sins of the penitent in Absolution. The sacramental life of the Church is henceforth not a theory, but an experience, and one which ripens as life advances, and in countless instances has endured the supreme test of the approach of death.

6. Belief in the Ascended Christ inspires a deep sense of personal responsibility. Few things are more necessary at the present time. In a self-pleasing, self-asserting age responsibility is apt to sit very lightly on many, or to be wholly ignored. Men and women, nay, even children, claim the right to be arbiters of their own conduct. This is so not only with the very rich, but with the poor and dependent; in all classes of society the question which men put to themselves is not, 'What is my duty?' but, 'How can I get the greatest amount of enjoyment out of my life? how can I best succeed in evading its burdens?' The same irresponsible selfishness prevailed in the Greek society of the first century, and the Church met it not with a mere system of ethics, but by preaching the ascended and coming Christ. *None of us liveth to himself, and none dieth to himself.*

For whether we live, we live unto the Lord ; or whether we die, we die unto the Lord.[1] *We make it our aim, whether at home* in the body *or absent* from the body, *to be well-pleasing unto him ; for we must all be made manifest before the judgement seat of Christ.*[2] So S. Paul taught, and so he lived. The constant thought of the Master behind the veil, who might any day appear and take account of His servants, inspired him with enthusiasm and kept him stedfast to the end.

This sense of responsibility to a Master in heaven is one of the most pressing needs of our own time. Men and women and children must be made to realize their relation to a Christ who lives and sees and hears ; who is the appointed Judge of all men, but especially of the household of God. The semi-pagan life of the baptized masses who regard themselves as their own masters, needs to be startled by the trumpet note of judgement to come which S. Paul sounded in the ears of heathen Athens. The doctrine of the Ascension and the Return must be presented afresh to our generation, in the sternness of its imperious call to a recognition of the claim of Christ over the individual life.

7. With the acceptance of personal responsibility to the Ascended and Returning Christ there comes the stay and joy of a personal hope. This hope is not less personal than the service : *where I am*, our

[1] Rom. xiv. 7 f.   [2] 2 Cor. v. 9 f.

Lord has said, *there shall also my servant be; if any man serve me, him will the Father honour*;[1] even the messages to the churches in the Apocalypse end in each instance with a promise to the individual conqueror. And it is a hope which beyond all other human hopes has power both to uplift and to steady the life on which it has laid hold. It uplifts the life of man to the highest level of which it is capable, giving to each individual a citizenship in heaven, a permanent footing and permanent rights in the greatest of all communities, the New Jerusalem, the City of God. And as it uplifts, so it is a steadying power in the midst of the tempests of life—an *anchor of the soul* by which we weather the storm, tossed like others who are not so anchored, but escaping serious harm.

There is perhaps no feature of early Christianity which is so seldom reproduced in the Christian life of our own time. We are busy with the social or the ecclesiastical questions of the hour, with the work of charitable or religious associations, with the side of the religious life which is concerned with the present order. When our thoughts turn to our Lord, it is of the Christ of the Gospels that we usually think; the Ascension has taken Him out of our sphere, and we scarcely try to follow; the great hope of the future, which was ever before the minds

[1] Jo. xii. 26.

of the first generation, has little power over us in the hurry of life. This change of attitude must bring some corresponding loss of spiritual strength, for which even the *work of faith* and the *labour of love* do not compensate; the *patience of hope*,[1] that reserve of invincible courage, which, helmet-like, protects the seat of the vital powers from injury, is no less needful to the soldier of Christ than the zeal which is ready to spend and be spent in His service. If it be asked how the primitive hope is to be revived in a generation which no longer regards His coming as imminent, the answer is, By the endeavour to follow our Lord in heart and mind into the invisible world; to realize His life there; to accustom ourselves to the thought that it is the life for which each member of His Body is destined; to bring all the engrossing occupations of the present, not excluding our religious energies, into relation with the Ascended Christ and with the great future which His Return will reveal.

The grace of God hath appeared, bringing salvation to all men, instructing us, to the intent that, denying ungodliness and worldly lusts, we should live soberly and righteously and godly in this present world; looking for the blessed hope and appearing of the glory of our great God and Saviour Jesus Christ.[2]

[1] 1 Th. i. 3, v. 3. [2] Tit. ii. 11 ff.

INDEX

Accuser, the, 94.
adventus, 131.
Advocate, 97 f., 100.
Ambrose, S., 121.
anamnesis, 47.
'anchor of the soul,' 102 f.
'ascend,' 6 f.
Ascended Christ, vision of the, 121 ff.
Ascended life, doctrine of the, xv, 3 ff.
Ascension, the, xi f., 1 ff.; doctrine of, xv, 3 ff.; practical teaching of, 154 ff.
Ascension Day, Ascension-tide, viii, 7, 85.
'Assumption,' 6 f.
Atonement, the day of, 42 ff.
Augustine, S., 111, 121.
authority of Christ, the, 21 ff.

Body of Christ,' the, 74 ff.

Caesar-cult, the, 19 f.
Christ, Person and work of, 156 ff.
Chrysostom, Prayer of S., 119.
Church, the Catholic, 71 ff., 158 ff.; worship of, 162 f.
Coming, the future, 129 ff.
Creeds, the, xiv f., 1, 6 f., 10, 72, 135, 140.

'daysman,' 91 f.
Diognetus, letter to, 160 f.

'ecclesia,' 116 f.
Epiphany, the final, 133 ff.
Eucharist, the, 46 ff., 118 ff., 162

Father, the revelation of the 60 ff., 111 f.
Forerunner, Christ the, 101 ff.

Gloria in excelsis, 121.
Gospels, their attitude toward the Ascension, xi f., 2.

Head, Christ the, 68 ff.; no visible head of the Church 73 f.
Hebrews, Epistle to the, teaching of the, 4 f., 36 ff., 95, 101 f
Hierarchies, good and evil, 22 ff
Holy Spirit, the, 54 ff., 100.
hope, 102 ff., 164 ff.

Incarnate life, the two parts o the, xi ff.
Intercession, 93 ff., 100.
intermediate state, the, 106 ff.
Irenaeus, 1 f.

Josephus, 41.
Judge, Christ the, 140 ff.
judgement, 142 f.; day of, 144 f. representations of the, 146 f.

King, Christ the, 16 ff.

life after the Parousia, 108 ff.

INDEX

'ligaments,' 76 ff.
'Lives of Jesus,' xi.

'mansions, many,' 104 f.
maran atha, 133.
Mediator, Moses as, 87 f.; Christ as, 88 ff.

Nature, relation of, to Christ, 26 ff.

'paraclete,' 97.
parousia, 131.
'perfect, to,' 107.
Philo, 41, 88, 92.
preparation, our Lord's work of, 113 f.
presence of Christ, 116 ff., 121 ff., 125 ff.
Priest, Christ the, 34 ff.
priesthood of Christians, 45 f.
prodromos, 101 ff.
Prophet, Christ the, 53 ff.
Prophets, the Christian, 57 ff.
prophetic office of the Church, 64 ff.

Reign of Christ, time limit o the, 32 f.
responsibility, personal, 163 f.

Session of Christ, 1, 10 ff.
spouse of Christ, the, 71.
'Supreme Head,' 73 f.
Sursum corda, 155.
symbolism, xiii f., 135 f., 146 f.
sympathy of Christ with the Church, 81 ff.; of the Church with Christ, 85 f.

Tabernacle, symbolism of the 40 ff.
Te Deum, 113, 153.
'Tent of Meeting,' 40 f.
Ter sanctus, 121.
Tertullian, 2, 56, 117, 127.

'Vicar of Christ,' 72 ff.

World, the, attitude of the Church towards, 160 ff.
Worship of the Church, 162 f.

www.ingramcontent.com/pod-product-compliance
Lightning Source LLC
Chambersburg PA
CBHW050806160426
43192CB00010B/1660